GENERAL PRAISE OF JEANNE BRYNER

I love Jeanne Bryner's poetry for the way it pulls me out of being lost in relentless abstract thinking and returns me to the real world of nature and people who know how to live and work in it. Jeanne sees and feels the actual world and also meanings and metaphors, and then shares her vision and her feelings in language that for me brings the world "health" to mind and then becomes love, of the most generous kind. Love, strength and beauty radiate from Jeanne's poems as, indeed, they do from herself, personally.

—Gurney Norman, author of *Kinfolks*,
and former Poet Laureate of Kentucky

ALSO BY JEANNE BRYNER

FICTION:
Eclipse: Stories (Bottom Dog Press, 2003)

ANTHOLOGY (co-editor):
*Learning to Heal: Reflections on Nursing School
in Poetry and Prose* (Kent State University Press, 2018)

ANTHOLOGIES (editor):
Safehouse: Women Living With Cancer (1999)
Song: Breast Cancer Survivors (2000)

PLAY:
Foxglove Canyon (2010)

REVIEWS OF JEANNE BRYNER'S WRITING

EARLY FARMING WOMAN (2014)

In this book the reader is teleported back to the earliest farmers in a time when young virgins are sacrificed for the harvest, a nomad woman must decide to abandon one child to save the rest of her brood, and violent raids are common to acquire or defend the best land. The images are brutal, yet beautiful, as the women of the poems braid communal bonds of sisterhood required to nurture life against the beginnings of war. Bryner has mastered placing her poems in a way that surprises and shocks the reader with story.

—Roberta Schultz, Teaching Artist and Performing Artist

BLIND HORSE: POEMS (1999)

Jeanne Bryner's poems in *Blind Horse* bear witness to the small miracles that add up to survival in the harsh, difficult worlds of steel mills and mines. She documents the going into, the going under—dark sweat trickling out the old dreams of a better life. She takes us into the workplaces, and into the homes, with an unflinching eye for telling details and telling moments in these lives. She is too wise a poet to simply celebrate these lives or mourn for them. These tough, hard-edged poems tell the truth.

—Jim Daniels, author of *The Luck of the Fall*

BREATHLESS (1995)

This is a fine collection of poems demonstrating the possibility of bridging the distance between the ill person and caregiver. The nurse becomes a companion, a witness who speaks out forcefully from the experience of suffering. She gives us these poems out of her need to share: "what I cannot bear to carry / alone / in the world." Two of these poems ("Butterfly" and "Blue Lace Socks") along with many other fine poems by nurses, appear in the anthology *Between the Heartbeats: Poetry and Prose by Nurses*, edited by Cortney Davis and Judy Schaefer.

—Jack Coulehan, MD

Jeanne Bryner is an emissary from the true world, and her book *Breathless* is a satchel full of direct experience and genuine compassion.

—Timothy Russell, author of *In Plena Vita: The Full Life*

Tenderly Lift Me: Nurses Celebrated and Remembered (2004)

Rarely do historical fact and poetry come together in celebration of both disciplines. *Tenderly Lift Me* skillfully combines the often tragic, always heroic lives of nurses with events of the past and present—our wars, social movements, diseases, and simple daily needs. The poems show restraint even as they burst open with passion. The accompanying photographs provide rich texture. Every library should have this book.

—Maxine Kumin, author of *Where I Live: New and Selected Poems*

Smoke: Poems (2012)

The poems in Jeanne Bryner's *Smoke* reveal her to be an angel of mercy not only in her work with patients but also in her ability to create poems that comfort and guide us as we face universal fears: sickness, personal and societal abuse, family tragedy, physical pain and emotional longing. Bryner intertwines striking images and perfect metaphors in poems that use nursing as a lens through which to view the world of healthcare as well as the lives of families, communities, and the art of writing. . . . Her poems dig deep, reaching what Emily Dickinson called "the zero at the bone."

—Cortney Davis, author of
The Heart's Truth: Essays on the Art of Nursing

Both Shoes Off (2016)

With a good reporter's precision and a gifted poet's empathy, Jeanne Bryner's latest book, focuses on "the epic of everyday life." Here, she recreates the story of her husband, her children, the roof and doors of her house, her unpredictable garden, and her farmer neighbor's crops and cattle. Beneath this deceptively simple tale lies an undertow of sorrow, as well as the frisson of joy and laughter necessary to sustain a long marriage, deep looking, and an engaged life. Like a contemporary Ovid, Bryner uses her considerable powers of metaphor to transform everything in these poems into something else. Here, gulls become boys, small animals become vegetables and people are trees. Even a tree's shadow "walks in stiff trousers." Haunted and haunting, *Both Shoes Off* is a true gift from a wise and accomplished poet, straight from the "good bones church" of her remarkable life.

—Maggie Anderson, author of
Windfall: New and Selected Poems and Founding Director
of the Wick Poetry Center at Kent State University

In Velvet

New and Selected Poems
1995-2024

Jeanne Bryner

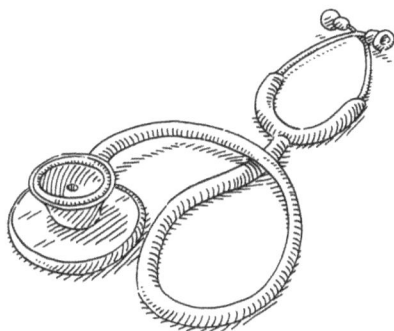

Bottom Dog Press
Working Lives Series

Huron, Ohio

Bottom Dog Press, Inc.
PO Box 425, Huron, OH 44839
Lsmithdog@aol.com
http://smithdocs.net

CREDITS:
General Editor: Larry Smith
Cover & Layout Design: Susanna Sharp-Schwacke
Cover Art: Susan Jacobs, "Homage to a Shirt"

Table of Contents

For My Brothers,

David and Ben

The death of the mother hurt the daughter into poetry.
—Lisel Mueller, "Curriculum Vitae"

I'd rather you come back now and got my stories,
I've got whole lives of stories that belong to you.
I could fill you up with stories,
stories I ain't told nobody yet,
stories with your name, your blood in them.
—Jo Carson, *Stories I Ain't Told Nobody Yet*

CARVING

I am not the first woman
to kneel beside opal river mist.

In my arms' basket, baby daughter is sky
her lips circle my nipple's flute.

Undone, my braids swish
tails of sorrel horses grazing in a field.

Back, back, my head tilts
while my mother, my daughter's

grandmother washes my hair.
Sun becomes a yellow blanket

covers us, warm; the baby's a loaf of bread.
She sleeps, our bodies glide

like waves over sand, softly mother sings
to the clouds. Our hands do the ancient dance

of morning. High above us, my sister perches
on her rock. Blade to wood, she carves the moment

quiet hummingbird, wren, golden eagle
the milk rising, the water coming down.

FROM

EARLY FARMING WOMAN (2014)

I.

I am the shade of a tree with many circles.

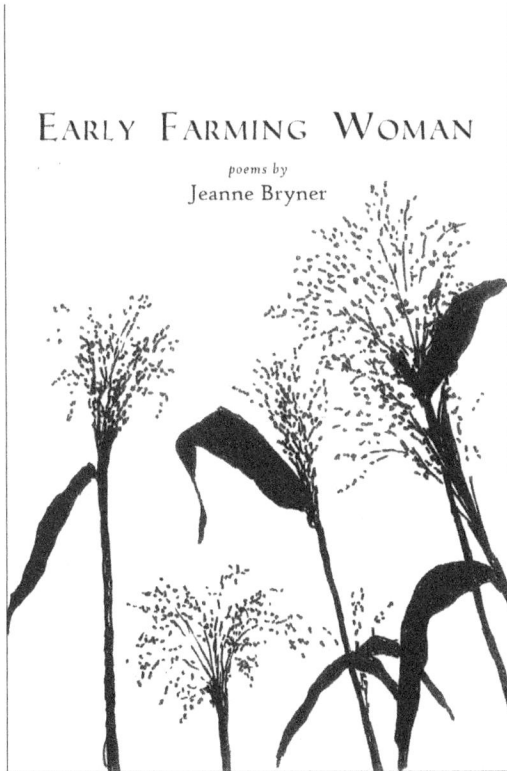

NOMADIC WIFE

He follows a voice I cannot hear.

In my man's arms, our quern cradled
heaped with cutting tools, scrapers, blades.

The baby cries and cries and cries.

I drag poles, skins for our hut, have no milk.
On the long march from the place where hills

slope gently up and first wheat was sown by wind
I choose a tree crotch to hold her.

As we walk away, she screams and screams and screams.

On my hip, her brother squirms, reaches for her
across the darkness.

I move forward, small fists find my face.
He bites my cheek. I let him. The blood runs.

His feet kick my belly where a new leaf quivers.
By this time tomorrow, we'll pass the grasslands

and the shepherd's holy rock. In another year
this boy weeping in my arms will be tall

old enough to work the fields
bring wheat for my stone

so I can pound and pound and pound.

First Blind Child

We live on the edge.

Because she has no eyes,
this back carries her

the way a tree holds
onto its leaves.

From an old pond
my sweet Lily, at long last

a song, a bloom. They tried
to drown her, but my

sleeping bear rose up
and ran. Three years now

just Lily and me.
Her voice brings the sun

her kiss makes our fire.
She sings every song

I know. Her feet and toes?
Quiet as moth wings.

Already, her hands read
deer tracks, scat, tree bark.

She can fish, swim
use her knife.

From a frog this swan
who takes my breath.

A butterfly, she pulls
our longboat away from death.

EARLY FARMING WOMAN

This is not the rainy season.

Across the river we eye each other
the dark-skinned man, a bloody lamb

slung over his spear, me with a basket
of seeds, my three children, hungry.

Near our village, water holes shrunk
to puddles, game driven off, bones

bones everywhere. Four moons ago
my man went with the others

following the scent of rain. He fell
from a tree, the wind left his body.

I have his arrows, a sliver of flint,
his right ear braided in my hair.

We live on land no one else wants.
The men hunt, the women gather.

From stalks, I strip the grain
with my bare hands. They are rough

as bark and seldom suffer.
The man speaks, and it is the sound

of morning birds. My children wave
to him, point to his lamb.

I am tired of dry seeds and praying
for the clouds to tell their story.

I've had my fill of beatings
carrying the elder's water in clay vessels.

Whatever this man wants, I will give him
and my children will eat.

Tonight they will sleep
they will sleep and dream.

BOWLS

First time I knelt beside one of my sons,
head bashed in, gray as ash

lips the color of field violets,
his father's face splattered, ranting, chanting

how many they'd killed — three hills over —
a tribe who kept women in caves.

Morning, just before sunrise

I gathered my gourds, filled them from our river
again and again and again.

I washed my son

soothed clay into every hole, bound his fine head
with leaves and braided grass.

Gentle, gentle

I rinsed, dried and put away every part of him
that was me: his black hair spools, his cupped chin

the blue and white bowls of his eyes.

GRAY BRAID

Like frozen raindrops
men came down all around us.

By her feet, one swung
my baby's baby, the rock

split her head. Because she
hit back and spit, they cut out

my sister's tongue. I packed
her mouth with webs and mud.

I am her blood. I am her blood.
My walking stick? I made two

good strikes before I fell. One
arm, a knee—broken egg shells.

They beat us through the night
but no knife touched my braid

for I lay still, very, very still
and it was not my day to die.

I am the shade
of a tree with many circles.

When I am stronger
there will be much to tell.

I am my sister's tongue.
I am my sister's tongue.

LAMB

It did not happen suddenly.

We were living in the hills
hunters pounced, mother was killed.

A man carried me, bleating, writhing
back to his village. I could not eat grass.

His wife nursed me. His children made
me their pet, kissed my black face

let me roam at will inside thick mud walls.
When they called, I ran to them, every pat

and hug a new link for my chain. There were others
like me who possessed amazing curved horns

refused to kneel like dogs. Wooly tantrums
are not tolerated. The pit's uncovered, the stubborn

driven past its edge. The spears are true, the effort
of lugging meat home, saved. Over and over, I was bred

to the smallest docile rams. The children grew
swinging clubs, pelting rocks, a sudden thud

I was blinded. Now if the great door stands open
I don't try to leave. Protection is milk

and love, a brand
not nearly as gentle as it sounds.

NO MATTER HOW MANY WINDOWS (2010)

II.

I was once a life unfolding
under the tender apron of a woman.

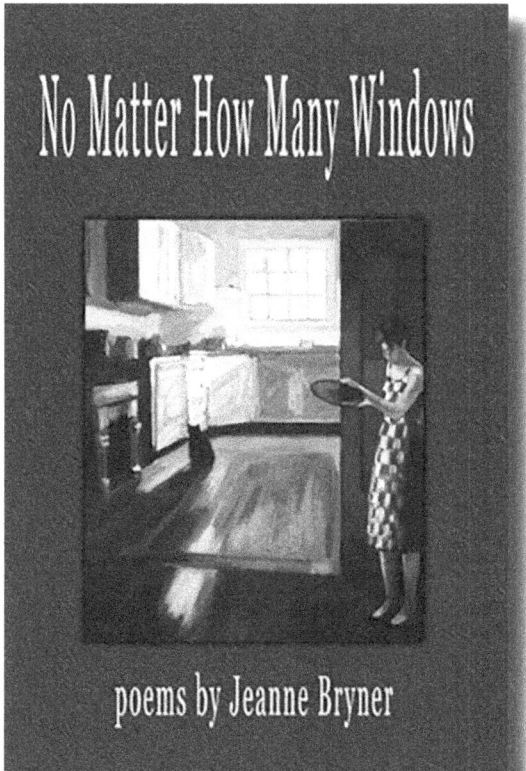

Rose of Sharon

I.

Begin with a rolling pin, a bobby pin
a safety pin or the pins we let others drive
into our hands and feet.
Here's what's at stake in the common corner
volumes of women's pale voices
bound and catalogued in the living room.
Do you have your card to this still library?

II.

Any moment, any day, we may sail off
the pasture's edge, so take a left by Lucy's barn
pass the pond; go to the forks of the road.
Make footprints in fresh snow or mud,
lift steel handles on any gate.

III.

See, sorrow lies in bales, tied with twine,
compressed and shaped, it's easier to move.
Feel the wind burn your eyes and skin?
It chaps your legs, whips your dress.
These are the fields of real women.

IV.

Leave your boots on the porch. Come in.
Behold her ivory cupboard, plain, plain.
See how she touches the flour sifter's cone?
Careful, careful. Even this becomes a sacred
marriage—when we choose the dance
our hands will do. Loaf pan, yellow mush
she washes her red hands, dries thumbs
fingers gently, gently. They are blind ponies.

V.

She opens drawers and cupboards, disturbs
the holy nap of empty space
the blessed point of every beginning.
Every day she draws the map of their world

the way it appears flat or round.
Do you think she needs a new linoleum?
It's anxious, curling up on itself.

VI.

She creates vapors, brings poultice
to the sickroom, paints scarred walls,
hums babies to sleep, shapes bread for her table.
Consider why she wants a double window
above her sink. Does she want the song of deer
running or the Rose of Sharon? Notice the drag
of her clothesline, how her legs grow stiff with age
icy as wood stumps. Should she cut them off?
Use them for oars? Is her body a house or a canoe?

VII.

She doesn't want us to answer the black phone
or sign papers which promise *lifetime rights.*
Stand by her fire, smell the bacon, the wood smoke.
Listen, she knows how far you've walked,
how tired you are. In this shade, please rest.
Do you like my Rose of Sharon?
It takes a long time to grow.
Come autumn the hillside is awfully pretty.
Those are pictures of my sisters and me.
Aren't we lovely and young in the frames?

Bertha Speaks to Her Great-Granddaughter

A girl child here is so much like an apple,
you must learn to eat the air. Honey, I lived
where hard wind blows, by a thread—you hang
there, singing hymns in a thin red coat.

I used to pray to be the teacher's gift,
the one bound for Snow White's lips,
but I am the broom of autumn that sweeps
patterns in her dirt, a branch of sweet grass

to mend baskets. I was once a life unfolding
under the tender apron of a woman
who canned warm sauce and baked pies.
By the time I held chalk, I knew seed

and stems, berries fit to eat or not.
Honey, long before I was a bride,
I heard talk of knives, being cored, hurt.
Smell the rot of spiral rinds heaped in my bowl?

That is grief, and we bury flesh, ashes
of any surrender, but I am here to tell you
you must name each bruised face
all the ones dried for dolls.

Yes, even the gnats drunk from cider
and the blessed worms
who'll surely carry us home.

No Matter How Many Windows
Bertha's Tenth Wedding Anniversary, April 21, 1908

Honeysuckle looks so pretty in the field,
pink and winding, smells better
than lilacs blooming in the yard.
A person just has to pick it up
carry it home. Finding a jar ain't hard,
nor dipping water from a barrel.
A woman becomes a man's bouquet,
but it's a chore to keep flowers alive.
So much handling in a house
no matter how many windows
there's never enough light.

WINTER THE COW DIED
CROSSROADS, WEST VIRGINIA, 1919

Snow drifts clear to my waist.
13 children wild as starved cats
prowling, snotty with colds.
Not enough grease to fix bub sop.
No man, no sack flour for biscuits
in the pantry. No dried beans
nor apples tied on a string.
Three half-rotted onions
and no deer meat hung
in the smokehouse. When
our cow took sick and died
I knew we musn't eat her.
I have brung in clean snow
played like it's ice cream
four days now, but their black
looks are hell's canaries. Jesus
says, *In heaven there's a bountiful table.*
Well, we can't cinch our belts
back one more notch.
In the barn maybe some
buckwheat's on the floor
if not, there's rope.

BOOKS

Nelly, I am Heathcliff—he's always, always in my mind—not as a pleasure, any more than I am always a pleasure to myself—but as my own being—so don't talk of our separation again.
—Catherine, *Wuthering Heights*

The trouble with only getting through the third grade
there is a heap of words on the other side a person
don't know. My oldest girl, Clara, were a good reader.
Many winter nights I'd ask her for a story
after the young ones were asleep. I'd pick up mending
pile, needle and thread. Over and over she read
the Emily Bronte book 'bout Heathcliff and Catherine,
how people marry the wrong person, buggy upsets
reins and horses get tangled up, only a moon for light.
I asked Clara what is a moor as they are all the time
wandering across them day and night.
It's like a field, Mama, she said. Clara—she can recite
and pretty too, don't mind to keep our secret.
Lord, it just broke my heart to hear it—so much hurt
wrote down by a woman, page after page.
Catherine dying, leaving her little baby girl.
Outside, December wind howled to come in
and across the foggy moor, two ghosts—
a man and a woman, still in love.

BLUE BIRD

He was from over around
Garrison and not ugly,
and me, ripe as a peach
aching for lips, dying for a kiss.

What we done in a buggy
tore petal from bloom.
You can't never be
a blue bird again.

Manure smell behind our barn,
in hay, I throwed up grits.
First time ever, I lied to Mom.
Corset laces cinched tight

as wire to locust post
for she grew like a tree
inside of me. The big sky. Jesus.
And Sunday's *I'll Fly Away*.

You can't never be a blue bird again.
Her and me? We crowd the nest.
Nights a crying on the porch
I watch maple, oak and birch

how they gray and bud and bear
—do nothing but quiet work—
only way they get to town
cut them down.

WEST VIRGINIA FARM, 1956
GRANNY CANDLES THE EGGS

Complete absence of wind, cricket song.
Over the shaft of evening
fireflies embroider a yellow cord.

Her voice is a chime, we gather
small hands to a washbowl.
Before sitting, she collects her tools

gray cartons, scissors for her string.
Mined from her hen house, a covey of eggs
ecru, ivory. Veined legs shuffle to her chair

all around us, darkness is mesh.
A light bulb glows inside the coffee can.
Rag in lap, she smiles, frowns,

wipes scuff of dung and hay hair
from her eggs. One by one, she holds them
near the light, shadow of yolk

strands of conception, magic and awe.
Back and forth, slowly she shows us
each capsule—a baby sun naps

inside the shell's paunch. She shakes
her head, sighs, some eggs put aside.
In a gingham apron, maybe

she's a fortuneteller, her coffee can
a crystal ball. Let the dining room
be a wagon, the string she measures

a mandolin. Let my grandfather kiss
her by the fire. Let me make her
beautiful with bracelets.

WHAT MAMA TELLS ME IN THE DREAM

When you get older (which I never did)
your ghost, your life flies into branches
becomes owl. This is the cruel meadow
of no sleep. Years I didn't tell you.

My wedding day, Dad threw a barn rope
over our farmhouse. It was July, pink roses
sprinkled near the porch. My satin dress
the color of sky, your father dashing

in his pinstriped suit. I walked to the North,
your father set out for the South. Each grabbed
onto the hemp. For ten minutes, we pulled
and pulled. Cousins, friends, laughing. Our rope

a roof's saddle, sliding slowly, going nowhere.
Dad fixed his hand near my waist, guided me
to your father's hands. *Now pull*, he said.
Of course, the rope came down. We didn't see

then the dark house of cages I carried inside
—how any jolt or bump might open them—
make me fly, a red-winged blackbird
through a terrible storm, a sweet elm raped

by a hurricane. In the land of Manic, I was queen.
All of you, my babies, my paintings, my subjects
—unharmed, unarmed. Often, there is no way to hear
the messenger from the other side. She has no drum,

no cup to pound thick cell's walls. My band played
and I sang. Take my white bones to set your table;
they are the good china. Wear my feathers in your hair.
When fire comes to your house, grab the paintings and run.

Found Poems: Mama's Letters

Today I am at home / writing poems.
　　　　　　　　—Alice Walker, *A Few Sirens*

I suppose you know we have moved
every direction you turn something to do.
I haven't had much help. It feels like fall
when everything is hidden. I took all the muslin
off the walls, there were scads of tacks—
when it's finished, it should look nice.
We made a driveway and wired the place.
Mom is sending cattle to the sale. She bought
eleven head of sheep. Sheep are real nice to keep
and make you more money than cattle.
Gerald's coming home for awhile
decided to enlist in the service. I don't know
if he'll pass his exam or not. He's going to help me.
He's going to tear these old porches off.
They are beyond repair, and I want them off
before the kids get out this spring.
They're really dangerous. I'll take some time out
to start my chili. I have it cooking now.
I was down to see Jerry. She's painting her bathroom
a real soft pink. Fern and Martha were up to see me.
We have our garden planted. It hasn't been fit
to work in. I'd like to have some little chickens
but I don't know. Please take care of the clock.
I don't know when I'll be able to get it. This is my
seventh month. We're hoping for a boy
the first part of June. Mom is fine. She has three
fresh calves. I get milk from her all the time.
People are tearing the old Stiles house down
board by board. I don't know if it's true or not,
but I heard Haywards were moving to Alice Wildman's.
You know George works away. Did your leg get well?
I hope so. Since I had Mary's tonsils out, she eats
better and looks real good. Martha White's making me
a duster out of red corduroy. Trudy sent me a pair
of blue slippers for the hospital. This is my seventh month.

We had a wonderful, happy Christmas. Write and let me hear from you. I have a telephone. 31F12, Hundred, short line. Love to all, Wilma

THINGS MAMA LEARNED THE HARD WAY

I don't like to remember bad situations,
up all night writing papers to get an A.
Mom's mended underpants hanging on our line.

Staying alive and paying bills is not
hitting the big time with Rock Hudson.
Eat hot popcorn, cheeseburgers, drink a Coke.

Keep turning the dial, find another station.
In high school, I was voted *Best Dressed*.
Mom sold lots of eggs, a hog to pay for my

senior pictures, things most women do.
She played harmonica. There's all kinds
of shiny earrings and lipstick, but you

have to know how to fix yourself up
without make-up, sort of show off what God
gave you, fiddle around to find a song.

I used to make up stories. When I died
they burnt them in a barrel.
Maybe you could write a little bit

about my life
there was nothing to it, really.

In Utero

From a sauce like rhubarb
I begin to appear slowly, slow
take away the peace of this place.
Mama, we share a sort of trance,
we share a soft water swelling.
You become my rocker on the porch.
I have the capacity for doing simple work,
but I swim all day, tug our rope for food.
I live in the state of being protected.
What a debt I owe. . .
thank you for the warm pink sea
the occasional white froth like lace in a stream.

SAUCER

The blind cat drinks from me.
I am a circle inside another circle.

Where the stone hit, I was born
and there shall I die

but not before making a little
clacking noise with my sister

and taking some heat. Someone
has to catch hell, small milky spills,

sweet brown drips.
It might as well be me

sitting quietly bearing coals
across my back.

I am what holds the brewed cup—
beauty to be broken, sighed over,

swept up and thrown away.

THE BREAD OF LONGING

Let us enter under a blistered white lintel
moving slowly, heavily, our arms interlaced.

Let the foyer mirror be ordinary—
your gray bathrobe, my mended flannel gown.

Let our pockets be filled with the paper money
of quiet mornings. Let us have one knife

and the strength to slice the bread of longing
on the kitchen counter. Let the table with its pale blue

chairs be bathed in sunlight for the old card game
of small talk, the simple fog of tea, the coffee's

darkness. Let us speak in syllables of settled debts
survival and unfrenzied corridors. Let our words

taste textured as aged cheddar. Let us unravel the silk
colors of knowledge, a smooth language folded,

saved by protective paper. Let us gaze in wonder
and surprise at the violet's fixed position of purple

the wind's sassy motion forcing gingham curtains apart.
Let us have a pencil and a bottle for this note.

Let us smile at the marked calendar of our best days.

BLIND HORSE (1999)

III.

Even if we say the lives of ordinary people
may be the dandelions, blooming, coming
always back, year after year
who will believe us?

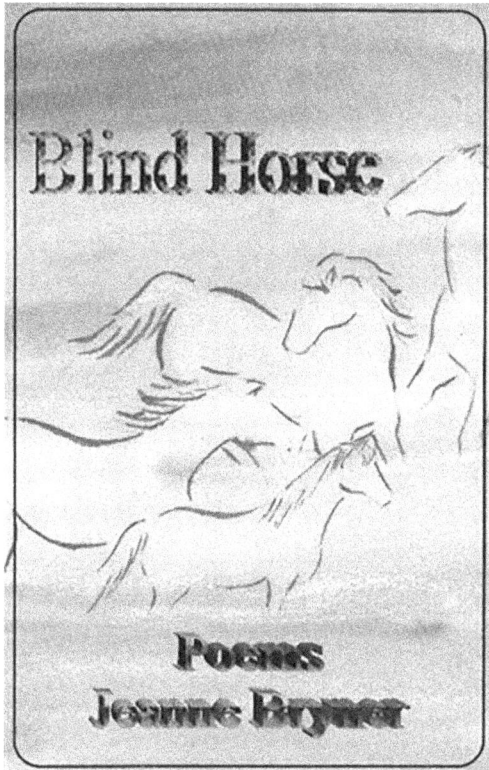

STONEHENGE

Our mill stands by the river
where all the men have disappeared.
In July sunlight, air hangs like a shroud.
Everything inside and outside
has come to a stop: furnace, pulleys, rails.

In the grass at my feet
gray rocks in a near circle
their roundness smooth as skulls
arranging themselves
bringing their hands up
to shield their sockets.

Coal Miner, Caples, WV, 1938

Consider this coal miner, who is still young
and blue-eyed, how he rests his jaw
in timbers of his palm, face dusted over
with what most shafts exhale.

Down the road you know there's a shot hole,
the place where he drags hope like a sledge
past the sun's pajamas, and pulleys lower
him in a wire basket.

Inside dark caverns, lessons begin.
His common hands follow glistening layers
of pigment to the middle ear of the mountain.
What does he hear in this immense labyrinth?

Does his heart complain that his shovel holds
no ruby, that air dances, a full-breasted woman
who spins her ether, drips juices over him,
a siren's song to make him stay?

He carries a silver pail, jam bread, yellow
cheese, coffee cold in a jar, the memory
of screech owls in the hollows of his boyhood,
where he runs, fearless, and magnolias hang

in pink ruffles, warm yams stick to his fork.
He tastes all of this, smells brown manure
falling from his father's mules. His vision
persists, a grail filled with morning stars.

Think of the way we are all porters, the weight
of picks slung over our shoulders, leaving
in darkness, morning after morning, the shimming
up of our thigh bones to hold us in stanchions.

Fatigue is a lean-to, days of garrets
furnished in quiet grumbles. Yet, we are rich
as this miner who scoops black honey
from a nettled ridge. We become the bear, rein
supreme in the starless land of tunnels,
where men with lanterns are kings.

LETTER TO WEST VIRGINIA
JANUARY 20, 1954

Dear Mom,

My belly's big as a wash tub. This one's a boy for sure—
kicks me night and day. I'll call him same as his daddy. Only
thing more tired than me is my elastic. For three weeks my un-
derpants act like Aunt Clara's parlor blinds. I pull them up and
two minutes later they curl down tighter than a new perm under
the south end of this baby. The burn is healing on Katie's arm,
just pink now, the scab fell off Friday. All morning Sam whim-
pered at the door. His water froze solid as a kiss on a frosty win-
dow. He could barely wag his tail. We let him into the kitchen
until Melvin gets home from the mill. There's nothing here to
hitch this blue wind to but skinny brown telephone poles. The
mill spits black specks on the snow like too much pepper on
mashed potatoes. I never saw the like of flat stuff, squeezed-in
families, hardly any trees. Winter's hanging on stronger than a
dead pole cat. Karen Sue and Lee Ann both have colds, coughed
until two this morning. I rubbed them down with Vicks salve
and hope to ride to the A&P tomorrow with Martha. I'm almost
out of bleach and cornmeal. Tell Lucy and George we ate the last
of the blackberry jam. Sure miss picking with Lucy on Pumpkin
Run. Kiss Dad for me and keep your feet up. I know your legs
have been swelling. Thelma wrote and told me.

Love, Mary Elizabeth

HOMESICK

Young men walked away from mountain velvet
to work Ohio's mills. Jobs were scarce
as hen's high heels back home unless you settled
for the mines, let your lungs stiffen black with dust.

Josh and Luke moved into the far end of our house
two rooms and a bath, home brew in brown bottles
and rag-tag kids to listen by their bare feet
while they hummed and remembered how blue

Kentucky grass grew, how salty West Virginia hams
hung, how Pennsylvania deer had bigger racks
and how they missed watching stuff grow. Hip pockets
bulged with Mail Pouch like their jaws. They yearned

to plow a field, put down seed and wait for rain,
wait for green. Summer evenings they'd hunt
four-leaf clovers, show us the way slender grass
tight between your thumbs made a sweet whistle.

The dirt of the mill ground deep, welded heat
from the shop made them thirsty. Weekends, not long
enough to get them back to Kentucky. Taverns
were handy and liquor eased the fever for the plow.

OUR FATHERS

The day Joe Brodie fell into the acid pit
they say he screamed bigger than Texas.
When they pulled him out, his legs slid
off his waist like melted red candles.

He was crazy—screaming for his mama,
his wife, Martha Jane and his kids all at once.
Just before he blacked out, he clutched
his foreman's stiff white shirt,

Help me Tom, please— my legs.
Joe Brodie died on the way to the hospital.
Our fathers finished their shift.
That night my dad, his best friend, Ted,

walked to Tony's Bar, got slop-the-hogs-
falling-down drunk, talked school days
back in Bobtown, PA, how yeast dough
smelled rising in their mamas' kitchens,

how many bales they'd toss in June,
how they missed those sweet, lazy
West Virginia nights, how hot Ohio
was, hot and flat, people called us *hicks*

and *ridge runners*, but by God, we knew
how to work. Our fathers never missed a shift.
Salt stains scribbled lines on coveralls
like small boys print their names in dirt.

Paper Dolls

Ed Grimm thumps some on Alice Ray,
onlyest thing we can hear is her crying
through the bathroom screen.
I dress Betsy, fold tiny tabs over her shoulders

around her waist and a bonnet trimmed with lace.
Alice Ray sits in her green kitchen, one light overhead.
The night's black as the walls of our coal bin, heavy
as lard. Ed Grimm holds his granddaddy's gun

to Alice Ray's soft yellow hair. My daddy walks fast
to Grimm's with Ted Wilson, Mama calls us
inside, our names break in the center like saucers:
Mary, Benny, Davey, Nancy, Lee Ann.

After bit, Daddy and Ed and Ted sit on our side porch,
fill it up with sprawling country-boy backs.
They pass a quart of warm home brew till it's gone,
smoke and chew, spit and cuss the mills.

Back home, it's baling time, ice water carried
to the fields in Mason jars, but here, in Ohio
it's lay-off season. Pink slips are gunnysacks;
men are kittens. We bend together or fall apart
like the dolls in my box.

SUNDAY MORNING

Mama stands blotting her red lipstick
and the tired bible waits on our gray
kitchen table. We have a nickel
for the collection plate and whine
because Ben gets to carry the coin.

Ben will drop it, we fuss. Mama is firm.
We wear strawberry pink dresses, the boys,
sailor suits. Bacon grease is mama's scent.

Nancy scrapes cornmeal mush into Sam's bowl
he gulps. Glass lies broken in the trash
and blood stains dry on our green couch.

Sunday morning means the end of Saturday night
pain. Mama buttons her aqua seersucker skirt.
She is a wave from the ocean. She presses
pancake make-up over her left shiner;
her ice bag sweats on the toilet.

My mama sings softly beneath her wide-brimmed
straw hat *Oh come to the church in the wildwood,*
and Mrs. Harvey points at my mama, the brown
suit preacher pounds his Methodist pulpit
screaming about hell's fury. . . .

My mama's hair is the color of honey;
she quiets my brothers. Her pancake make-up
melts from all this talk of hell.
Her left eye is a slit under a purple avalanche.
And purple is the color for the church,
the color for royalty.

Page Seven, Lee Ann's Baby Book
July 12, 1955

Willy Mackley welted your back with a stick.
I marched you straight to Sue's—welt
and tears and dirty knees.
Willy lied. Sue held him. You walloped
him right in the mouth. He won't forget
salty taste of his own blood. Sue and Myrtle
and I had lemonade about noon. We know
Sue did right. We don't hold with our boys
hitting girls.

Number One

It was the day for making the number one.
A white-haired woman walked her first grade classroom
the blue dress girl drew calligraphy ones: a curve
on the left side, a tiny base to stand on. The white-haired
woman stopped, said, "Make straight lines; that is not a *one*."

The blue-dress girl had seen the curved
number on a bottle in her mama's hand.
She loved her mama and the curve swooping up
like a bird and its base for the bird's perch.
Her page became a tree filled
with soft swooping *ones*.

She was so busy drawing *ones* she didn't see
the hand coming to slap her across the face.
Diane Bailey turned and gave her a tissue.
The white haired woman grabbed her *ones* paper,
crushed it with her slapping hand.

She handed the girl a new sheet of paper.
Row after row after row the children's *ones*
lined up, straight as bars across their pages.
The white haired woman smiled.

A woman with brown hair sits at her writing table
remembers her blue dress and hot tears.
She tells the story of ballerina *ones*—they hold hands
and dance—baby's breath in their hair, satin slippers.

Degas begs to paint them; they refuse.
They dance in leaves and snow and hay. They dance
and dance and dance. And when they grow tired,
they fly from her page like gray mourning doves.

APPLE CHUNKS

I remember that day in the second grade
when I knew for sure my mama'd never be well
enough to bring in orange juice and oatmeal cookies
for Halloween parties like Kathy Hawkins' mama
who had shiny gold hair and smiled all the time
like an angel on a Christmas card, 'cause my mama
couldn't think to feed my baby brother or take her
yellow medicine or get herself out of her pajamas
before my daddy came home from the mill.

That's why Doc Mason said she'd have to be *committed*.
She'd been gone almost forever, and when I thought
about her, a chunk of apple caught in my throat.
I nearly couldn't breathe. Daddy divorced Mama
that same year. I reckon he was tired of her sickness.

In May, Aunt Haddie took a gall bladder attack
and my cousin, Ruth Ann, showed her three stones
in a mustard jar. One was big as an acorn. Luella
Donovan had a breast cut off for cancer (we never knew
which one), and Janet Porter's mama had her female organs
removed when we were in the sixth grade.

All these women came home sickly pale from ether,
then one day you'd see them at the A&P
laughing by sack potatoes, their cheeks pink
as strawberry milkshakes. I don't figure my mama
bought a slab of bacon by herself after I was nine.
I hated Doc Mason and my daddy.

Last winter, Kathy Hawkins told me her daddy died,
buckled up tight with a heart attack, which is easier
to take than brain sickness. I wrote her pretty mama,
Mrs. Hawkins, a card and told her I was real sorry.
It is the hardest thing in life to chew gritty oatmeal
cookies and drink orange juice with apple chunks
stuck mean in your throat every bony day.

HOW STEEL SHAPES OUR LIVES:
GRADE TWO, ARLINGTON ELEMENTARY

Our teacher, Mrs. Dillon, raises
the square, white screen.
It might be a sail wanting wind
or our mother's pale sheets
trying to dry in January.

This is Ohio, 1958
our third year away from West Virginia
and the forsythia by the farmhouse.
This is assembly: gray chairs, a movie
about *How Steel Shapes Our Lives*.
We are small, our hands folded.

Mornings of walking to the barn
with my grandfather are far away.
Still, lambs crying for dead mothers
must be bottle fed. I know it
and know how, when they suck,
it feels good to pet their wet faces.

Mr. Jonah makes the room go dark,
then, he flips a switch: magic, magic.
A light warms the reel's black film
upside down numbers flash. We hear
a big voice without a body.

We have been taught to sit and listen.
The movie makes us feel like we're beside
the men in hard hats, where yellow dozers
gouge the earth, take what they want
haul it to our mills for processing.

This is the inside of a steel mill, the voice says.
The men move like shadows on the screen.
These are the stories given to children
evil trolls beneath the bridge, to cross over
someone must pay a toll or be eaten.

This is a blast furnace, the big voice says.
We don't even know what that means,
but a pink glow settles on our faces
as the ladle vomits its river of red steel.
Sparks spray the men's coveralls, hands
and hair—men who look like Tom's father,

Debbie's father, my father, so I whisper
Run, Run, Run, and rub my Bible-school
Jesus pin for luck. There's so much noise
in the mill, the men can't hear me.
They wear their iron shoes
and keep walking through the fire.

WHAT HAPPENED IN THE FIRE DRILL

for Mrs. Amy Davis

Gypsy Lane, snow past father's Buick bumper,
Mama, her hospital gown, again, crying depressed.
Doc Mason mumbles, *give her three shock treatments*
and *No, I don't think she's pregnant.* Inside Mama
my baby brother's a tadpole, a secret afloat in a pink ocean.
The lightning zaps him, snaps him, slaps him. He tries
to swim away. The cord wraps his neck: one, two, three times.
He dangles, waits to be cut loose, grows heavy. Raggedy Andy
hangs himself on a bloody noose.

Blue baby, incubator, *we don't know if he'll live.*
My grandmother says name him from the Bible, call him
Benjamin. My folks, numb, press the nursery's glass.
Mama cries; father holds her hand. Doctors say *cerebral palsy.*
Ben's cerebellum's a drunken cowboy in town, a Saturday
night that lasts forever. Pabulum chokes him, he can't sit alone.
Dish towels strap him in the maple high chair until he's four.
He bites his tongue, likes strawberry ice cream and bananas.
We all carry him. When he runs, his feet are broken paddle wheels.
Bobby Ford calls him *retard,* gets a willow limb across his butt
when we tell his mama.

First grade, Ben sits, patient at his varnished ink-well desk,
hair shaved close, green pullover, wide eyes of a fawn.
He repeats numbers, colors, slobbers, wipes his chin.
Stars in the flag. He stands, covers his heart.
Outside the long windows, every year waits; the football field's
shoulders lie pinned by heavy goal posts.

His teacher smiles, slim in her lavender suit and light pearls,
straight like Ben's teeth. Her chiffon blouse exhales White Shoulders
White Shoulders. Ivory pumps and sable hair set in a French twist.
She's Lady Bird Johnson, chalk dust on her nails
lesson plans and apples on her desk.

Ben squints, no end to his papers' blue lines.
No letting up. No pause. The trick: get letters to land
between these lines. He knows this. He's seen
his sisters dash from the yawning school bus waving
math exams, spelling tests, manila sheets full of gold stars,
red A's. His pencil becomes a black frog licking
his squat fingers and spastic hands. He bites his tongue;
it's an anchor, a weight to make his B stay put.

Fifth grade, row three, Mrs. Barrick reads us
the *Little House* books, raw blizzards, how families survive.
Her voice feels like the hearth in their sod house.
And I think orange flames dancing. I wonder
how Ben will ride out a fire drill with a drunk cowboy
in his brain. I imagine him tumbling down the stairs
trampled by polished Buster Browns, dirty saddle shoes.
I'm way up here where Laura's sister's going blind.
I'm on the second floor. I can't see Ben or carry him.

Fire drill. A wail like a man with a nailed hand.
I run from those prairie stories, fly down the hall,
remember smell of hair burning. I want to save
my baby brother who cannot run, who is not a retard.
I slip past the fourth grade teacher's clip board,
trip on a number two pencil, hit the gray steps
two at a time. When I round Ben's hallway, breathless,
I see his head bobbing like a sand balloon above
the lavender shoulder of Mrs. Davis
while she carries him
                    down
                         every
                              single
                                   step
in those ivory pumps—his lead-smeared palms
rubbing her chiffon blouse, his saliva
glistening on her pearls.

Delivery Men

They did not look
like our steel mill fathers
those white-nailed men
who rang milk bottle bells
smelled like incense
lowered cardinal red flags
on hushed gray mailboxes.

They did not sound
like our steel mill fathers
those honey-humming mailmen
and willow-whistling milkmen
who passed cool, sweaty bottles
light bills and sweet bird talk
to our melon belly mamas.

They had tidy names
sewn straight
on their ivory soap shirts
right over the left pocket flap
and crisp brown pant legs
buffed stallion black shoes.

They had racks
for clear, curved glass
pouches for stamped letters,
and their names flashed
like medals in the sun.

And our gingham mamas
smoothed floured aprons,
tucked stray hairs
and June bride blushed
when they came—smiling
every day—
delivering their parasol shade.

Ice Cream

Summer steeped and pulled
the sky blue ice cream truck
to our side of town where kids
were sand and money was magic.

We'd hear its wind chime song
grow stronger as it kissed the curves
of every block. We could taste vanilla
buried under bitter chocolate,
sweet melting sugar cream frozen fast to a stick.

Summer steeped and pulled
our fathers to hell's oven
at the mill, and we all got angry
because that brazen ice cream truck
still came, still came day after day.

It still came knowing that sweet dream
stuff, that fine cool flavor
was out of reach
for our gingham mothers.

Summer steeped and pulled
its trigger with little bullets pressed
to little brains. It was the sky blue
ice cream truck, a wind chime song
growing weaker as it kissed the curves of every block.

WHERE GOD LIVES

It is hard to believe in God, even now.
He was always somewhere else. Maybe fishing.
And sometimes I get mad. Like when my sister
was eight and I was six. Daddy went drinking,
left us all alone with my baby brothers.
We were potty-training the chubby one, Ben.

I went to pull him off his potty seat
and his weenie got caught in a crack
of blue plastic. Blood spurted as if I'd chopped
a hen's neck. My sister ran. All four of us crying
now, and me, holding Ben's poor wiener
like a bloody worm in a washcloth.

I begged God to stop warm ooze soaking
through to my palm and held Ben
who yelped louder than Sam the day
we shut his tail in the closet. *I'm sorry,*
please God, help us. I chanted my prayer
the way you do when you see the train's face
frothing in the tracks, its yellow eyes and teeth
hissing the dark and your car's stalled
all the doors locked tight.

Our screen door whined, slammed
when my sister brought the women
in their calico blouses. They found Vaseline
in our cupboards, rocked Ben until he slept
gave us an orange popsicle, threw
the potty seat in the trash.

It is difficult to believe in God, even now,
but I want to say, that day, when I was six
and holding what was left of my brother's dick
in my right hand, God's hair was in pin curls
under a red bandana. He had two names
Elsie and Janet May. He lived on our street
the four hundred block in the projects.
He was home. It was August and too hot for trout.

64

TRAINS

Kathy's house was white, two-story,
had black shutters, sat next to the tracks
and a patch of orange poppies.
When the trains came through, they grabbed
her house by its shoulders and shook it.
Our girl bodies trembling from those wheels.

Kathy, her sister, Rose and I were shaking
her three brothers rattled, her mom's
breasts jostled and Rebel barked softly.
Then Kathy would open one sable eye and say
I really hate those damn trains.

But, I rode those heading-somewhere-in-the-
night thunder trains, imagined French speaking
lovers kissing good-bye at moonlight stations.
I loaded cattle-smelling cars with stubble-faced men
whose sour breath played sweet harmonicas.

Lying beside my best friend, trains moving
our covers, I dreamed a twinkling city filled
with goat herds, a sleeping hamlet at the ankle
of the sky, a city where love was a candle burning
in every window, a place where mothers
were pretty as poppies and children were butterflies.

I made a city that didn't breathe through
the nostrils of a steel mill, a town that didn't smell
like rows of slaughterhouse hearts,
a place where men could wrestle night to the ground
and drive their bursting lives as far as the brush
would paint, as far as the violin would cry.

Rank and File

Most toxic substances have their origins in
the workplaces of America.
        —Report, Ohio Environmental Council

Once hired, I became an apprentice
in survival. It hurts to breathe in here
the air's metallic, heat's a harness
rubbing every neck.

There are ways to suck the spirit
from people. How can you teach men
dignity and creativity when the boss
says, *make them dump the chemicals*

into the river on night turn?
So many fires. It's hard to tell friends
not to drink, but in a steel mill
your physical life depends

on the right moves of other men,
and doing a good job's not enough.
The owners want it faster, cheaper,
more gold spun from mud.

Struggle never melts. My wife's
pregnant. I dream water, our son splashes,
happy, warm in the sink. Bubbles.
Bubbles. I have no impulse to change

the world. The men talk retirement,
how they'll *live then*, fishing, humping their wives,
making wine with their own grapes.
Every night we stampede to the time clocks.

Georgia wants a house, a garage, a picket fence.
This job may get them, get me. I'm union,
my hands know the give-and-take of grease.
We are a colony of men feeding one furnace,

don't make us die in our boots—
we've earned America's apples.
Forty hours, vacation, pension,
the right to live long enough to grow old
and not be wretched.

ART IN THE MILL

From the beginning you must believe
it hammers in silence, has its own routine
of faith, even the smell of a cigar

might become a poem, or a man's reflection
in his lunch pail wearing a hard hat
cast some light. Because a flannel shirt

draws warmth from a man's trunk
you must acknowledge his soul possesses fire.
In the kingdom of coveralls, you have to imagine

pines, a forest where it is Sunday forever,
a clearing so full of morning you want to pray.
There's nothing wrong with pretending ore pellets

are grapes ready for dancing feet or a huge vat.
Communion flowers everywhere.
Because a tow motor is the exact yellow

of mustard seeds, you must pay attention to the fields.
Because art whispers, you must listen and trust your eyes.
Once, I visited a steel mill, a rare thing today,

all the men seemed hopeful
their hands and faces
covered in sculptor's dust.

LOURDES

Where be all his miracles
which our father told us of?
                        —Judges 6: 13

There were rumors
if the men took pay cuts
gave up sick time and vacations

shaved some insurance benefits,
our mill might be spared.
We waited for a sign.

The blessed mother did not appear
on the project playground,
and when Mrs. Cavelli cut her palm

slicing pepperoni, Father Conko shook
his head, said that wasn't really stigmata.
Round the clock women in babushkas

prayed the rosary. Candles burned
in rows at St. Michael's and St. Joe's.
All that smoke and incense,

still, not one statue wept.
At the union hall, some of the men
came drunk, cursing. My father (who never

spoke before a crowd) stood up:
Don't give the sonsabitches nothing back.
We worked too damn hard to get what we have.

Let the bastards close her down.
We waited for a sign.
The next day they hung it on the gate.

PIECEWORK

When times are bad, you can do it at home.
The pay's low, but hunger's a good thing to know,
to remember. Plant your garden even if the bombs
are coming. Take shit from no man.

Be a rag sorter; follow the horse-drawn carts
with two wheels. Faith is the main thing.
Carry hope on your shoulders like a saint
for feast days. Mix Dago red in the coffee

for nights of picket duty. A decent wage is worth
the beating. Slow down, sit down, walk out
on any speaker who says, you *have no right to go back.*
When you grieve, take the person with you,

your father, mother, the forty-year-old woman
who died paralyzed from working too close
to the freezer all those months
in the bacon-finishing department.

She had kids. Be willing to go to jail for an idea
about justice. A log driver says to loosen a jam's
dangerous, it can cause death, but a stopwatch
can be a gun, and a man is not a machine that works.

Don't forget the last days, your father
and the men stood around the gate
singing labor songs, wondering
what they'd do tomorrow.

Blue Collar

You must change your life.

—Rilke

We know, we surely must know
there are moments before explosions
before any body count, when breaking
windows and screaming might have helped.

Serious bargaining over the old contract
human dignity and ruling by fear.
No simple answers exist,
but when they tell you, *They got greedy;*

see, now it's all gone, it's all gone.
What they really mean is, *It's okay*
to let some furnaces go cold,
some children go hungry.

Did your teachers ever make you memorize
the names of coal strikes? steel leaders?
tell you the story of the Triangle Shirtwaist Company?
the chicken factory in Hamlet, NC?

Learn the Gettysburg Address,
the Pledge of Allegiance,
the Preamble to the Constitution;
study hard and you may move up.

But the rules are the rules,
justice doesn't wear a flannel shirt.
Without the working class,
what is America? What is America?

Where are the great studies of buried miners,
burned women, displaced steel workers,
the lost towns gutted like deer,
people left to choose between the river and the sky?

ANYTHING IS POSSIBLE

You can make the story different
the smooth tires abandoned in the lot
—where your house burned—
they can be your brother's church shoes

shined and waiting to be laced.
So what if the mailbox is gone?
Let the pine tree be Mama's green couch,
those two beer cans, doilies for each arm,

that covey of pebbles, baby teeth
swapped for nickels in the night.
Let the curved puddles of water
be your sisters whining as knots

were brushed from their wet hair.
Move from the center outward—see,
the coal furnace becomes less grumpy,
your father's blue cigarette haze

is a white candle lit for absolution.
Go slowly, reading every sign for pardon,
the unraked leaves are kittens wrestling,
the found nest, Ben's first birthday cake,

the wet newspapers, oval throw rugs drying
on the line, high in the maple's branches
those caught stars are Davey's kite,
the moon, a cup of cold milk and your mom

saying *Nat King Cole's all over his cancer;*
I'm so happy.

BREATHLESS (1995)

IV.

So much depends upon the needle hitting
each blue vein as though it has tapped a living tree.

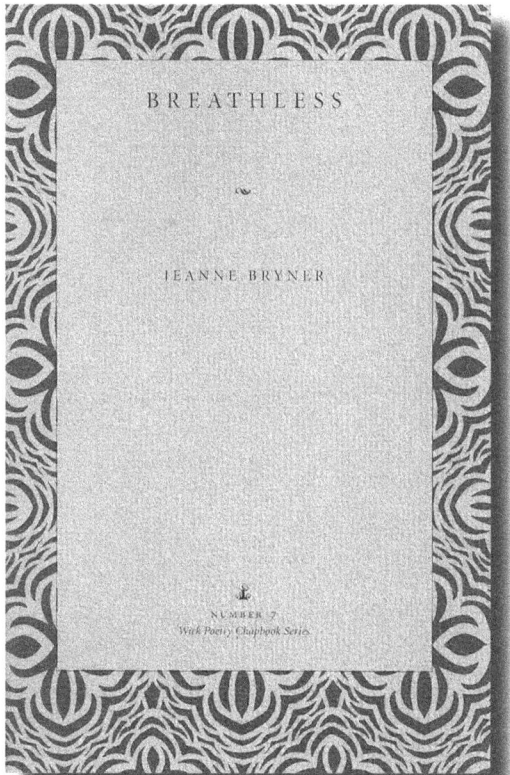

SIDERAILS

Dr. Stanislaw, did you know
second-year nursing students
are only permitted to speak
when asked a question,
attempt venipunctures
if veins resemble sewer pipes,
and make rounds holding hands
with head nurses?

Second-year blue uniforms
have the bath down pat,
can figure doses, write care plans
instructors then scar with red slash marks.

One Friday morning I made rounds
with you and Miss Kitch on 6 East.
A family member asked you to please
inform your silver-headed patient,
Miss Farley, they could not possibly
care for her any longer, and a nursing home
was the only answer.

We pulled the curtain. You lifted
her flowered gown, exposing
a sagging yeast-dough belly
now held fast with black suture
railroad crossings, a penrose drain—
everything healing well.

Then, your hands gripped
her cool side rails, knuckles white:
*Your family doesn't feel
capable, the best place, where you'll get
good care, a nursing home after you're
discharged from here.*

This was the dirty work
I didn't know surgeons had to do.
I think damp rails may snap
your bent knuckles are blanched so
—your voice slices syllables—
steady, scalpel thin.

You wish this molasses quiet
were a rotten-meat gallbladder,
a ruptured spleen, anything
you might cut away.

Miss Farley weeps,
soft, Baptist tears.
For an eyelash moment
you hold her hand.

On hairpin ceiling track,
shushed curtain slides;
Miss Kitch sniffs, cradles the chart,
and I want to tell you—something,
standing under the pure white and black
clock hands weaving our gray lives
into honest shawls.

I'd like to say, *Man, that was a shit deal
and you have class, Doc,*
but I'm a second-year nursing student.
You are Chief-of-Surgery.
No one asked me for an answer.
I'm just here to learn
how 70% alcohol and ten Hail Marys
wipe silver rails clean again.

For Maude Callen: Nurse Midwife, Pineville, South Carolina, 1951

I speak of a woman, blue black midwife
Of April fog, flood, swamp, and July nights
When Maude Callen's hands layered newsprint
In circles as a weaver works her loom,
Slow, to catch blood straw, placenta, save sheets.
I sing kitchen lamplight, clean cloths, Lysol,
Cord ties, gloves, gown and mask; she readies all
For this crowning, first mother, purple cries.
I sing of sweat and gush and tear, open thighs
And triangle moons, ringlets, charcoal hair.
I sing sixteen-hour days, Maude's tires bare.
Mud country roads, no man doctor for miles.
I sing transition, collapse of mountains.
Crimson alluvium, the son untangled.

BLUE LACE SOCKS

Three nurses work on the child
in the center of the bed. A little girl.
She is not yet dead. When we ask her to move,
only her chest rises. It is unbearable to watch.
My flashlight shows her pupils spreading
like pools of oil in her iris. Her curls are yellow.
Without thinking, I smooth her bangs
across her forehead. Her tiny body is silent.
I want to put my arms around her,
tell her we are all terribly sorry for this,
and the farmer who hit her will be caught and punished,
but I don't. The doctor says, *She'll have to go*
by helicopter. I walk her glazed mother to the desk;
she signs forms. I try to buy time
with only coffee money in my pocket.
I am aware of hanging bags of clear fluid
and listening for the whisper of her blood pressure.
The copter's blades: Thump, Thump, Thump, Thump,
Thump, Thump, Thump, Thump.
This noise should wake the dead.
But it doesn't. The flight nurse waves
through her window. I bite my lip and pull the sheets.
The child's blue lace socks hit the floor, like petals;
and their echo drowns the copter's blades.

BIRCH CANOE

for Captain Dan Suttles

After supper, my daughter asks me,
Any bad stuff today?

I would like to tell her *no*,
but she's seen the six o'clock news,
yellow tape surrounding the trailer's shell,
the story of sisters playing with matches
our fire captain, tired, begging parents
to put lighters up, install smoke alarms.

She knows the child named Sara
came to my hospital.
I am touched by her concern,
Will they make it, Mom?

I try to tell her about the fireman,
young and sweaty and mustached,
his scorched suit
kneeling beside our gurney,
holding swollen sooty fingers
of a toddler he did not know,
praying for this flower he'd gone
into the flames to gather.

I try to tell her
about men who are gentle and strong,
men who rise without hesitation,
become larger than themselves
and do not paint their faces
with arrows and do not thump
their chests blue.

I do not know
how they tell themselves not to be afraid,
how they let the black smoke
swallow them over and over.
I just know tonight this fireman
was a birch canoe; he swam into the fire
and pulled Sara back into this world
that is never easy.

Letter From Ward Three

I.
I am busy today watching my ceiling crack grow
green in plaster. My hands fold over the collapsed
melon of my womb; this is where my five babies
floated like pink letters in a mailbox. I remember
doctors in the delivery rooms, postured shells
in olive gowns, slapping the child until he found
his voice like a fingernail against the blackboard.
They are all that became of me, ribbons and shoelaces
that bind me to corners of rooms where it rains
yellow trees and paper cranes beat their wings
forgetting where it is they wanted to fly.

II.
I had some nice things once: a wedding band,
lavender stationery, a black lace slip. I held
clothespins in my mouth, tasted clean wood,
hung diapers in neat rows.
My fingers sifted darkness like sand on a beach.
Maybe you think I will die; I am weightless
as an old movie on the screen. I urge myself back
over and over—through steel wires like miners
feeling their way through tunneled cave-ins.
I am harmless as the back door of a valley,
quiet as a gray plow horse pacing unclean tiles.

III.
There's a tied storm rising in the gulf. Thinking back,
I forget the man's face buried among the babies,
the owner of giant fists, the climbing on and off,
the milkman's sandy smile, my broken picture of Jesus.
Blood on both sides of my table, winter,
a piano with no song. Naturally, I believe the boats
will come for me or I would never invent footsteps
falling close in the night. Once, I was young,

a woman with enormous eyes; the thing about living
is hesitation—the snowflakes saying your name,
the leaves gossiping, and the sun telling you
it is easy—that bread is better than hay
that everything that needs you is real.

BUTTERFLY

The thing I keep thinking is these young men
are much too weak to make love. These boys
with yellow hair and blue tattoos and bristly
mustaches who are married and dying with AIDS

cannot enter each other the old way—bony hips hang
unbeautiful, too tired to pump. Like soft cow bells
their hoop earrings tinkle in ER, room thirteen
as they press cool cloths to foreheads, pass tissues

for sticky green phlegm. They wait for the doctor
and lab techs and nurses who mark their plastic name bands
with a *B. B* for *blood hazard. B* for *boys. B* for *bad.*
Orange-ball stickers tag their charts; flags go up that say danger.

I am their nurse; when they ask for blankets,
they cover each other the way I spread quilts
on my daughter in her crib. They are half a butterfly
on gray cement, their skin shrinks and tarnishes

bodies cave in, revival tents collapsing the final week
of summer. They cough as I enter their room
and something in me stiffens. Even this far away
in my mask and gown and gloves trying hard to say—*I care*

that you suffer, that your cottage burns—its flames
reach inside my tent. Whatever chokes in this fire is large
and soundless and pale. I keep thinking as these men lift
each others' heads from the pillow gently tilt straws

close to dusky lips, hold hands as needles dig for veins
and pull and straighten hospital sheets hour after wounded hour—
they are migrating back to the cocoon, the place
where brown masks protect the unbeautiful.

VIOLETS

In the hospital's emergency room
there's a girl with enormous eyes
and shoestring hair who puts razor
blades on her tongue, in her vagina
month after month.

She lives in a country
where there are no prophets.
Our longest bridge of candles
will not lift her to the bridge
over this black river.

Any meadow needs flowers in it
or a small girl dragging a red sled
while her dog jumps beside her.
A child wants cocoa waiting,
dry socks folded on the bed.

Consider this girl,
saving her razors like ticket stubs.
What makes her believe
the razor's kiss can heal a life
battered as a sparrow?

Nights they bring her to us,
dull as a gray rag, we wash her
the way you'd wash a mauled terrier.
And when we close her skin
with suture, scars blossom pink scrolls

—rows of azaleas—like nothing
you can smell or taste, like little girls
in their eyelet sundresses
running toward you
their fists full of violets
crying, *Here, here, love me.*

BREATHLESS

Dear Trent, today I was remembering the clay faces
of parents pulling red wagons in Akron's pediatric hospital
and a three-year-old girl named Ashley with a brain tumor
the size of a melon, that pale train of four-year-old boys
pushing their IV poles like Sisyphus with his rock day after day.
Maybe you can't recall me, the fumbling nursing student
with hazel eyes, gripping her pink spiral notebook, who mixed
enzymes in your applesauce. You drew me a picture that July,
1978. And it was splendid too: your Mommy, her jeans and blouse,
her boyfriend, Luke, on his Harley, the one Mommy rode
on weekends when she missed visiting and your beagle, Sam,
wagging his tail by a single blue flower. You handed it to me,
pointing wildly with your clubbed nails: *That's my dog, Sam.*
And that's my house. That's where I live. Here, keep it.
It was awfully cold that summer, and you didn't tell me
what to do with this painting you left behind.
Please listen. The oaks in my neighbor's pasture are awash
today with autumn's blush, and on some island, sandaled
monks are praying for war orphans, and me, I cradle
almost everything: my daughter's baby tooth, the smell
of apple fritters in my granny's kitchen, this faded manila
paper filled with crayola marks. In the next room, Kenny G
is playing "Breathless" on his sax. Wherever you are, Trent,
come sit with me in his horn's amazing shade. I know
now it's wrong to want more than this scrap of paper,
sinful to rescue angels.

This Red Oozing

I'm a nurse in emergency.
You're a hostess at Benny's Lounge,
thirty-five, divorced. After three beers,
you can never let the friend of a friend
drop you off at your apartment,
ask him in for coffee.

Never pee with an accountant in the house,
especially one dragging his briefcase.
See how the balding sheriff shakes
his *I-told-you-so-eyes*—
while you tell how the man shoved
your bathroom door open,
pulled out his revolver, grinned.

We know what he said next; we hear it
nearly every week: *I'm gonna fuck you;
you scream, I'll kill you.*
We believe you cried, begged on knees,
told him your kids might be home soon.
You kneeling on the fuzzy pink rug—
he likes that—you genuflecting.

The safety clicks on his forty-five.
You know guns; your father hunted—
black roundness against your right temple,
your hoop earrings clang, train whistles
in your ears and his words squeeze:
suck hard bitch.

We're sorry, at how the doctor
makes you say it all again,
how a single lamp burns on the night stand
and your kids smile in their school pictures.
How tight he holds the cold muzzle to your neck,
jerks your dark hair like a mane and rips
you until you bleed, your breath becomes
grunts, your face in a pillow.

Doctors in ER speak like priests.
They try to explain it, clean it up
when they swab, hunting for sperm, trying
to mount rage on slides—dead or alive.
This red oozing,
this trail from your buttocks to your thighs
will not fill him, and it doesn't matter
how many times you throw up green
or call on God or bruises rise
like small iris on your cheekbones,
the razor moves on.

The friend of your friend
with the pinstriped suit will probably walk.
I think you know that.
What you don't know is how he rapes you
endlessly: how he crawls out of your lipstick
tube in the morning, slithers out of the soapy
washcloth in the shower, snickers every Friday
when you dust those photos on your stand.
How his boots climb the back stairs
of your mind year after year
as he comes and comes and comes.

Tenderly Lift Me:
Nurses Honored, Celebrated and Remembered (2004)

V.

Say, there was blood, I carried water.
These are my hands. I am not Jesus.

Becoming a Nurse

My arms lift up as this drunk man stumbles
toward me. He claims to be an FBI informant,
demands two x-rays and the truth
about Kennedy's assassination.

I can barely keep my balance in this dance.
He circles our emergency room, a broken boat
cursing the moon. This far inland
we cannot hear the gull's cry or feel the wave's fist,

but I can see his family: four sleepy toddlers
clinging to a hollow woman harnessed to him
in her wrong-buttoned dress. We are all in motion
and the bow aches under our weight.

It exhumes my smashed tea set, mama's bloodied lip,
little girls learning that women must clean up
earth's magma, the kinetics of sweeping linoleum
after the bomb, the pressure of hunger and combat.

This is the way the heart pulls forward
to our life's work. We embrace something endless
like sand. We wash and floss the wrecked ship's hull
and its seedy sailors who are always arriving on our island.

The Labor of Tenderness

Dear Mom,

Yesterday I took my daughter, your granddaughter, to work. I'm a registered nurse, twenty-one years. With my own money I bought her shirt, an olive vest with covered buttons, wheat-colored trousers with French seams. Her shoes cost $20.00 (on sale). And yes, you're right about spoiling her, but she's my daughter. She shouldn't traipse the emergency room in faded jeans, dirty sneakers. Her hair's the same as yours; it is the color of honey. She took temps with a computerized thermometer. Yeah Mom, numbers click so fast it makes the patient dizzy to watch, then, there's a beep like a bird singing. Twelve hours she was beside me, the full shift. It wasn't like summer days with you—handing clothespins in our yard—hoping the winds might come, the rain hold off until the final load. I tried to lead her easy. She was close, eager to please. Like those first times you lifted me to hang diapers and Dad's red hankies. When the first man came with a swollen ankle, I helped her fix an ice bag. We have plastic bags covered with white cloth, Mom. And crushed ice falls neatly from a silver machine. It wasn't like Sunday morning, me emptying stale bread from a sack, climbing the gray chair to fetch fresh ice for your black eye. It wasn't like rooting our junk drawer for a gum band, tying the sack off like an umbilical cord. No, it was neat and clean. Four snowy ties to secure it. She watched me order x-rays when I suspected a fractured *navicular*. Mom, I know how to spell navicular. And it's okay to order x-rays. I do that. Before any doctor sees the patient, I make a decision. Alone. And my daughter was with me. She palpated pulses on either side of a wrist. In the afternoon, I showed her how to set the wheelchair's brakes, how to steer a person without hurting them, avoid sharp turns, go slowly. Mom, a lady came in vomiting and she held the basin, said, *Ma'am, here's a chair, please have a seat.* Gentle as a stewardess. It was nothing like a week of five kids having flu in one bedroom. The vomit glistened and was a similar green, but it was so civilized and orderly. Nobody weeping over the mess. Mom, she saw a man, his finger dangling, a factory's press; her voice reassured him. *My dad has one cut off too.* Yes, some things are the same. Children in our valley still learn their father's body may be given up, but Mom, she believes in her father, believes he is a mountain, wants to go to work with him next year. She has blue eyes, Mom, not anything like our brown. Remember how story problems gave me hives? She does algebra with a pen. Mom, we wish you were here. We're having a great time. We're doing all right. Your girls are fine. We're just so damn fine.

LEARNING THE BODY

after Florence Nightingale's Notes on Nursing

The heat of the body must be examined
by the hand from time to time.
Brush knotted hair, hold people close
at night, children, foul persons.

Be terrified of all methods, very rarely expose
the breath and bodies of the sick.
In your apron carry spoons sticky
with the sun's honey.

Guard against confusion, remember Socrates
and become the quiet pulse.
Entered into sleep, men and women evaporate
into themselves, into the air.

Flesh fades, a wine-soiled dress
every seam needs repair.
Be motionless, think this: where is the tea
yellow lotion and writing paper?

The little house burning down is a beggar
passing a bad night.
A door opens, it is a fever
speaking in tongues. All night, people hold

close, children, foul persons.
Learn the body in the bed, any sore
red gauze damp as poultice
not suddenly, not in a rush.

Say, *There was blood, I carried water.*
These are my hands. I am not Jesus.
Make the story a song.

To The Place of Orchids

Father Damien, nurse to lepers, Molokai, 1864

The best orchid is small
and lives far away from the world.

What do I remember? Two men, dark as crows
in a field, cutting rows with their hoe.
Slow and sad, like giant tree frogs
who come out at dusk to climb skyward
the way prayer flies, unstoppable
toward heaven, knowing there's no hope.

Because of lost feet, one man had climbed
the other, who had no hands.
I felt my arms grow stone still, and my feet
fat against the grass. Brown hood and vows,
I sailed here, wanted to serve people
who would not look up.

Back and forth, row after row, peas, peas,
peas falling like rosary beads to feed
this village of fetid angels dressed in rags.
I stayed, lived in the middle of it, orange
blossoms, pure as virgin's breast,
palm trees, perfect in the wind.

The sea was behind me, and I changed
years of bandages glistening with sap,
taken down every day like wires from their
limbs, sweet bodies ripening, rotting
like pieces of fruit in a bowl, and me,
trembling under God's white, white clouds.

Some days, I wanted to scream,
Where is the sacred table and bread?
No Bible verse rose like bird song to help.
Caskets waved like lilies in my dreams.
No way to resist the Savior's shackles
to our ankles, our hearts.

I stood under the moon, doing my work,
told them to think orchids, nothing
but orchids, what we were, blooming
in this island's terrible sunset,
where we died, coming closer.

A peasant's house, the kitchen table, candlelight
All night the men work at her body.
Stiff as a plank, she is hard to undress.
Villagers claim a priest fathered her child.
Shame drove her to the river; she rose
After three days, a salmon with silky hair,
Her baby's fists still clenched inside.
She feels, somehow, softer when the knife opens
The white cage of her breastbone
And warmer when they spread her wide.
Their hands are a meat cutters: bloody and crude
They drink wine to make it easier
And try not to see her hair spilling
Like ink almost to the chair.
Until dawn they hack and cut and lift.
They place the heart and fetus
In separate sacks, smaller than pillowcases
But clean, very clean. Because she
Was not a criminal, what they've done
Is against the law, but Leonardo's an artist.
They drag the woman to their cart, dump her
Back into the hole. Her arms flop and twist
And snap under her hips.
She cannot cover this huge emptiness.
They shovel the earth upon her, dirt,
Dirt, dirt, and cold, like brown pearls.
Now Leonardo draws her heart's chambers,
Each vessel's breathless chimney,
And her baby hugging his bent knees.
Art takes everything, digs for secrets,
Ravages the queen's tomb to seize her gems.
It leaves nothing in the unlit house,
But silence and stains upon the floor.

Miscarriage: The Nurse Speaks to the Baby

We are going back to the dirty utility room
you floating like a ballerina in a jar, and me
wondering how you found an open space in the woods.
Little gardenia, you have split your mother's heart.

To make a baby for this world, women spin
a film of scarlet cobwebs inside themselves;
they ask a blessing, to become a gourd,
a field where grain is grown.

You are the dancer whose rhythm is not metrical,
and I name you *abandoned flute*.
You are the tiny globe of two worlds, and I hold you
a pale candle too wet to light.

You are the journey unwilling to go forth,
watercolors touching the sky, spices
from a faraway land, daughter of silk and air and dawn,
vine of warm ground born to suffer loss.

JUBA

Helen Albert, retired nursing supervisor

Not the gray truck bound for the cotton fields
or thirty-mile mornings dark riding cold,
not the sweet biscuit smell twisted in Mama's hair
or the dull flowered dresses stretched
to cover bare legs. Closer and closer,
our coats were whispers, straw hats frayed,
hands literate in the energy of motion.

Not the oval slowness of filling hundred-pound
sacks or the backs' silence wanting to walk away,
not the soft hymns singing themselves across
hired rows of squatters. No. Not the mechanics
of stops and pauses, day labor without shade,
but the clean taste of water from our own jugs,
the sense of purpose given to those who work.

Not the parlor chairs or starched linens
or cherry staircase of Dr. Maritn's, not waiting
on his porch for my three dollars. No. The day
he went to Norwood Hospital on my behalf,
the Monday I was one of eight black women accepted
for nurse's training. Yes. That afternoon, and the Sunday
Mama's best friend, Hannah, pulled white sheets

from her bed to sew my uniforms. The coal miners'
paychecks handed over by my uncle and brother
to buy my nursing shoes so I might have the power
to lift the raw material which was my life.
I'm seventy-six years old, and at this distance
the pieces come together, one thing embraces another,
clover fences and creeping grass, suppers of salt pork

and warm beans over cornbread, wooden ironing boards
holding the dead until a box was built. Me, learning
hard lessons of science and logic, finding the narrow strip
of light where God lets everything grow,
how I graduated first in my class at Norwood,
a black woman in Alabama in 1943,
at the southern rim of Appalachia,

Not sailing as far as the Cape of Hope,
but a place where the growing season can be long,
and girl, you must be glad for rain, straw layered
around the community of jars in the storm pit,
any old cow still able to give milk.

Hope Chest: What the Heart Teaches

Dear Heart,

For her science project, my daughter has chosen you. She's
asked for my help. Four boxes are on the form. I will need assis-
tance: *some, a little, a lot.* I have a *few* supplies. Her teacher's letter
explains the problem need not be large, for example: *think why
the family cat claws the sofa.* My daughter is thirteen, the age I was
when the Beatles arrived, put girls into screaming fits. The three
survivors (George, Paul, Ringo) are making a comeback, though
I'm not sure why. Why reinvent the sixties: Kennedy in Jackie's
lap, the endless bloody war? My daughter's tracing the vena cava;
she pauses, *Does it ever stop before we die?* And I'm reaching for an-
swers like a can of pepper. I want to tell her about that first dance,
the old gymnasium. There was a boy: short, polite, thick glasses.
He asked me to slow dance; we moved chest-to-chest. It made me
dizzy, a little short of breath. Something not governed by reason
had me, a journey began. I passed from one place to another. Do
you remember, heart, how that sweet boy moved away in July, his
father transferred? How you taught me to sacrifice cargo, lighten
the ship's load? Heart, please notice how carefully she colors her
graph on bypass surgery. *How many attacks can one person have and
survive, Mom? I believe it depends on the person and where the damage
occurs. Some places in the heart recover easier, but the heart is never
the same. I mean, there's scar tissue forever.* Did you hear that heart?
Look at this science project scattered around the kitchen, books,
helpless before the steamy breath of my fried chicken, pages
describing your constant bath of warm fluids, the coming in,
going out, vessels like ivy vines embracing your pink cottage, its
four small rooms. You have lived the soft forest, a rose, an apple,
radiant in your crimson dress. No prince could reach you, chop
you down. Out here, leaves burn. Every day is a torn jacket, worn
lapels; wind and sand slap the sclera. We feel the random move-
ment of jaw bones and floor joists. And what have you planned for
this child printing her note cards on resuscitation and brain death?
Today, I'm wearing my favorite skirt, the one with deep pockets,
a wedding band, my sweater's on the rocker by the desk holding
my daughter's baby shoes, some paper, this pen. I'm going into
the next room to ride the stationery bike, ten minutes or five miles.
Be ready, ready for anything; comb your red hair, smile.

After The Battle: In a Room Where We Have Tried to Save a Life

The curtain is pulled; it's time to lift the oxygen
from the nose, be careful of the hair's cilia.
I hurry to turn off hissing of hoses and machines.
I have been here before

wetting a white cloth for the face, sliding down
the jaw's crease and landing in a neck filling
slowly with lavender. I am lost in a glacier
of glistening spittle and the mouth

surprised in an "O." I am afraid of the undressing,
how the arms straighten for a gown of blue flowers.
I have been here before
washing the hands of a man and thinking of my children

on busy August days. Falling, falling. There is not time
to clean out all the palms hold. The black wheels turn
as I wipe gel from the rib cage, trace a burn mark
on the chest. I want to kiss it. I want to kiss it.

Once, long ago, I would know where to gather roots
for a poultice, how to kneel and be forgiven.
Another face enters the room, a woman.
Together we roll this trunk, these four limbs.

I have been here before
Sour breath of warm stool mushrooms inside the buttocks.
I hear the sound of running water and throw
the body's mud away.

A final sigh or moan comes after this.
It is the wind and not a complaint. There is a strange land
ahead. Here, take this pillow for its dreams.
I am afraid, so I talk about rain and a trip

we may take to Scotland—how the grass is tall there
and the music pure. The man's journey has started,
and I'm looking to see if I can tell anything about the road.
I have lost something

in the business of heart scribbles and paper strips
curled upon this floor. I toss them like confetti.
Once, long ago, the needles were swords
and the man was a knight, maybe a king.

His blood meant battles for a god, for honor, a country.
His spirit is a hawk circling. I have been here before
crying, picking up heads on the moor
knowing it is done.

November 1963

B.J. Panchik, nurse, occupational health

The girl I was sits on the kitchen floor,
moves her father's rag undershirt back
and forth across her mother's nursing shoes.
Where mother's foot had been, I slide my hand,
feel how her weight has stretched the leather
each sewn part grown to fit her toes.
Some powder she sprinkled inside drifts
its dust into the air. I pull the silent tongue
see how the laces have crossed themselves.
Her heels suffer their slants. This close
I cannot escape the layered smells of sweat.
I am eight years old, third grade,
and already I have learned how blood dries
a rusty brown, how it freckles her shoes,
stains her uniforms. Tuesday's my night
to shake the pale liquid and smooth it on;
halfway down each shoe the leather cracks
a gray scar from so many missions.
With the rag's soft ribs I rub and rub and rub
until the white's like the satin sash
on my communion dress. In two weeks
we'll wash the good dishes, polish silver,
hear a wishbone's snap after the turkey's carved.
In Dallas, our president will be shot
and for days my parents will stare
at the TV set and each other;
newspapers will be saved.
A small boy will salute a flag-draped casket,
and my sister will have her turn shining
our mother's shoes—a ceremony
thanking her for every step of her life.

What Nurses Do:
The Marriage of Suffering and Healing

Jane Ball, retired nursing supervisor

Compared to the day I had to sit with a mother
Ask for her daughter's three-year-old kidneys,
Eyes, liver and heart because a drunken
Teenager had killed her brain
Compared to the afternoon I told a black man
His son was shot while jogging
Compared to the night I was paged to ER
To help sedate a seven-year-old girl
Before they sewed her crotch.
Being here with this schoolteacher holding
Her husband's hand, begging him to live
Is better.

The rhythm of a heart repeats itself like vows
In a chapel full of light, but we are gathered
Here because this man's heart choked after forty years
Medics shocked him, brought him back
Then, a cardiologist with his pacemaker, a respirator
We have stolen these minutes
But our bag has no more tricks, no more drugs
Or gizmos, and now, something as old as love
Must be the pencil to help the heart write
Good-byes across our screen.

I will never forget the wife's brown hair
Her tan corduroy blazer, how her eyes glistened
When she asked for her husband's baptism.
We couldn't reach a priest. It happens.
I said I could.
In the presence of this company
Who gives this man to the next world?
The paper cup was blue; I asked a blessing
For the tap water and did it; water fell
Soft as a kiss to his forehead.

And so I kept the devil far away
And let the wife cry into my shoulder
For a long time after
For a long time after.

BEGIN AGAIN

for Lynda Arnold, nurse HIV positive

They meet bent over to drink from one stream,
faces close as apples on a branch
mountain water so cold their teeth ache.

Tenderness, his forehead's purple mark is gone,
some granny's hand has patted it back to earth.
A nurse, her patient, they are not strangers.

She blushes from this closeness, the bodice
of her gauzy dress touches each breast.
Opacity, the origin of forms, his new body

so tan and full, cotton shirt blown open
in a breeze. *Warm day,* she says, smoothing
her hair and staring at the meadow

holding its bouquet of wildflowers like a bride.
He nods, kneels, jeans faded, pockets walletless.
Smell the pine? he asks. She shuts her eyes

breathes the sap's blue jazz.
Every day thin needles die and drop
a symbol to begin again, to find an answer.

His fingers lift her hand.
Is this where my needle caught your glove?
She nods, sits down.

Do you remember the snow, she says,
how it fell on your face softer than sugar
then melted like tears?

Yes, yes, he answers. All around them movement
organza skirts of poppies, flushed and twirling
lacy parasols—a dance, a waltz.

Silence, a pause before the starting line.
What do you miss? They ask each other
speaking slowly, knowing it was an accident

meeting there, here. The question's a wound,
a drop of blood no longer visible.
Their words scatter across the fields

so small we cannot see them.
They float through the air saying *nothing*
nothing, singing forgiveness.

HOUSES ARE BURNING, BELGIUM, 1915

Edith Cavell, World War I nurse, executed

Write it on plain paper; use a pencil.
Three officers burst into my class,
when they bound my hands, my students screamed.
Tell that the soldiers were German;
they marched me to a cell smaller than father's study,
walls dirty mule brown. There was a blanket,
a basin, a window the size of my family's Bible
in Norfolkshire. Tell them it was August, summer
worn out in a wrinkled skirt and I was English.
In the margins scribble, *She spoke no German.*

Do you believe history counts houses burned?
Lives lost? Then write my mother's name, Louise,
say her geraniums and ivy bloomed in crocks
by the rock garden. Remember to say my father
was a minister; he wanted my sister, me to be apostles,
pull a ship full of hungry faces across the water.
We became nurses. Belgium asked me to train
their nurses, and I wanted to teach.

People were being killed. Write it.
And write how we built a hospital, one hundred
seventy-five beds. Tell how soldiers came and died.
My nurses tended them like wrens nesting in a thunder-
storm. The armless were shaved, the wounded dressed.
My nurses were young and wore sadness like ribbons
in their hair. Write about the orphan ward,
how I would go there every night, alone, one hour
lift the most restless, hum lullabies I'd heard above
my pram. Write about England, my country
filled with coal mines and poets in unmarked graves.

Write this. Soldiers took my white apron and blue dress,
handed me old trousers and a shirt. I rinsed my bloomers
out after my evening meal with what was left: my drinking
water. The soldiers never reached for my breast;
they spoke softly. Write about the boy-guard, he walked
stiff-legged, had a draining wound. Tell how I bandaged him
and he gave me soap. He might have been my son.

Write it down. Get it all down, how a man came
to our hospital; his eyes begged like a squirrel
caught in a steel trap. He said Germans would not
suspect a nurse, Belgium was neutral, the Allies
needed men. I agreed to help, hid soldiers and men
in our hospital. At night, we ran through narrow
streets like rats in a sewer; there was a tree
in the woods, I whistled a signal. Later,
once or twice, letters arrived.

Do you believe blood turns a stream red?
Then write this. I cut my hair with broken glass
and drew a calendar on the wall. Late September,
my bloomers glazed with frost. One morning the prison
chaplain visited, told me my nurses drafted a petition
for my release. They risked their lives by signing.
They were young and wore hope like a locket
around their necks. Get more paper.

Write about my trial. There was an interpreter
because I could not speak German. Thirty-five
of us were tried in two days. My barrister told me
there would be time for appeals. He spoke French,
a language I learned as a girl. French sounds like
the brook on my grandmother's farm, china cups
in mother's kitchen. Tell them I had hope
and read silence like scripture.

Write how soldiers stood by the chaplain
the last afternoon when he said my sentence was death,
but would surely be appealed. We prayed, took
communion; he left. Then, the boy-guard brought
lemon tea cake, hugged me, pointed to his leg's scar.
After ten weeks, I loved him, this boy, who might
have been my son. Tell them it was 1915 and people
were dying. We were chewing off our legs to get out
of a thing bigger than England or Belgium
or the careless sky spilling its every star.

Do you believe all this happened? Still happens?
Then write on. In darkness, they bandaged my eyes,
covered my head with a veil. Walking to the wall,
I noticed one of them limped. German words clawed the air
like a garden hoe's clack. Rifles coughed, cleared
their throats. Please write this.
The soldiers refused to fire. An officer's bullet
split me like an olive. I saw geraniums—red, red,
red—and mother's ivy blooming in crocks. I was English,
here to train nurses.

Interview With Sister Denis
of St. Joseph's Hospitallers
Colony of Montreal, New France, 1694

Three months after the new hospital burnt down.

—Your family is in France?
—That is true.
—How many novices started with you?
—Twenty.
—How many remain?
—Five.
—The rest?
—Took husbands in the Colony.
—I have heard stories of trappers with frozen feet and scalped
     men crawling to the fort.
—That is true.
—And women found dead from childbirth in their cabins.
—Yes.
—And this is where you sleep?
—Yes.
—Isn't this the cellar of the granary?
—It is.
—But sister, the partitions are rotting, and here, see the wind
     pushes snow from all sides, surely the rain—
—We sleep back to back.
—But a good gust could take this ceiling. And the roof being so
     close to the floor—
—We pack the cracks with rags and straw.
—Sister, the brown loaf on the table? How are you able to slice
     frozen bread?
—We thaw it on the hearth.
—Is it true there was a fire?
—Yes.
—And your patients?
—Most of them jumped through the windows.
—And the sisters?
—They ran into the hospital garden.
—But it was winter and night.
—Yes.
—And was there ice? Wind?

—Yes.

—And did they have time to dress?

—They were in night garments.

—Shoes?

—No.

—Stockings?

—No.

—Your patients?

—Those who lived were taken into the seminary.

—The sisters?

—Were given hospitality by the Sisters of the Congregation.

—The habit you are boiling?

—It was Sister Dominic's.

—The habit on the table cut into squares?

—Was Sister Helene's.

—The habits that are draped and drying?

—Sister Anne, Sister Catherine, Sister Marie, Mother deBresoles.

—They are bathing?

—They are dead.

—From the fire?

—From the sickness that starts with a blush and fever, the purple
    rash that turns to pus.

—And you?

—I bled them here at the temple.

—And the priest?

—Confessed the dying.

—But I heard the supply ship also brought typhus?

—That is true.

—And the bodies of the dead were in piles?

—That is true.

—And the sisters fell ill in great numbers?

—That is true.

—And then?

—We accepted the offer of service from several good widows.

—Sister, those flea bites on your hands? Will you be going home?

—Soon, I will be going home.

In Praise of Hands

That they are slaves.
That each tendon's a rope
and the knuckles are pulleys.
That their white bones
line up like pieces of broken chalk.

They are bound by flesh
as leather around a Bible.
That they dance and write
in air the story
what is lost, what is gained.

That they are soldiers
cut and bleeding, a link
to the heart's kingdom.
That they are so beautiful
a moon has landed on each finger.

That they are trained
for harps and hired for murder.
That the cuticles are shaped
like soft horseshoes.
They contain rivers.

That the ring finger's shyness
suffers when gripped by the powerful.
That the palm yields to blisters
and wears the calloused rags
of repetition.

That they are mythical
with their lifelines' hieroglyphics.
That they struggle
because of their great strength.
They are able to heal themselves.

That they know what it means
to draw the water
and work without pay.
That they will hide our eyes
and pray for our sins.

That they may lift the hammer
and lead our bodies to grace.
That they will make a print
like no other
until they wave goodbye.

.

SMOKE: POEMS (2012)

VI.

*Come to the table thinking where we might find
water, drill new wells, how many acres to be planted
this year and the next. Part of nursing
is learning how to die; you may want to turn away
but nothing must be forgotten.*

Bed Bath

Into morning's sacred space
our backs bend like saplings
in the wind: the nurse
to her washcloth
the surgeon to his scalpel.

It is one of the holiest acts
to set a steamy pan of water
upon the over bed table
to dip and dip your cloth's
whiteness and rotate the soap.

Disrobing the bodies
of the sick, adjusting limbs
and blankets, spreading arms
like wings, both people bow
their heads, become naked.

The hands need no
instruction, for here
palms make a path of swirls
like a wolf circling high grass
to shape her birthing cot.

The small talk of water's
splash is ancient, ancient
also are the brown spots
under each breast, the halo
of hair 'round genitals.

Let us remember our boats
await us; luminous cells
and salts ignite as fire
only to burn out
in blue basins, rest as hazy
light over a distant marsh.

STRAWBERRIES

Sometimes, walking for hours through my shift,
I don't feel the old man's weight on the gurney.
I don't hear the endless rotation of dirty black wheels
against this floor. I don't know how many pulses

I've taken at the end of the week.
The god of water comes to me, calls me,
and I'm a small girl running under a garden hose,
my braids glistening in its spray.

I want to say don't bother me, my Mama
has sent me to pick strawberries, fetch the cream,
and yellow cake is baking in our kitchen.
A man appears in the doorway clutching his chest,

his heart's a maple gray and twisted in a storm;
his breath becomes handfuls of raspy leaves.
A boy now, he gathers them, hands them to his mother.
I go to him, the way I'd just go to anything pale

and shaking, the preacher's wife fainty in her pew.
I hand him my art, two gloved hands, tired feet,
my simple row of needles.
Today, I want brown bouquets

to be the geese returning year after year.
I want it all to go on dancing,
tall grass sweet and hidden
in the marsh, every single wild strawberry.

NURSE AT THE TRAUMA CONFERENCE

I'm scheduled to read after the medical examiner,
just before lunch. Where I am on the dais—a lucky spot.
After sandwiches and cookies, the crowd
gets sleepy; they work 12-24 hour shifts.

Firemen, paramedics, nurses and docs.
The medical examiner's saying *Please*
you must be more careful with evidence,
more mindful of what gets tossed or saved.

Someone, he says, *threw panties away*
(it was a rape). In his sweater vest and bow tie
he might be an aging professor just off sabbatical.
He's telling us how long he's been on the job,

how many parents still practice
the fine art of child abuse, how before he ties
his apron, puts on his gloves,
brings his saw from its place on the wall, he prays

to the god of bones, the god of secrets.
He bends close to those babies and children,
curls his crooked pinky to theirs.
Show me what they did, he says.

I will tell your story.
I will try to make it right.

BREAD AND WINE:
POEM FOR MY BROTHERS

There was a backyard swing set, children
stabled, holding each other, driftwood in sand.
The stepmom was a snake, her venom choked,
reshaped us, platoon of servants, puppets unfold-
ed. We grew quiet, we never sang. Neighbor
women hung diapers, had their own shoulder's hurts.

Why make more smoke from what was not your hurt?
Men rode the mill's tremble, wives felt children's
foreheads. On the 700 block, five summers of sand
piled up. My brothers, ages four and six, choked—
bedroom inmates—chase their tails. Stick arms unfold
from shirts, pale as candles, heads shaved. Neighbor

women taught bedtime prayers, saw t-shirts. Neighbors
heard what was tied behind July's screens, voices hurt.
Bed sheet ropes dropped from a dorm fire. Children's
jeans, underwear on lines, but no boys. Hour glass sand
inches through. They made a field without green. I choke.
Baseball, team of two. Lengthwise, a spelling book folded

christened *bat*, turned inside out, cotton socks folded:
ball. Dave pitches. Ben strikes. They run fake bases. Neighbor
women heard, wiped their eyes, offered to call CSB. It hurt
to tell them *no*, but what tent welcomes five children?
Soft as rafter mice they ran. Any noise? The belt, sand
with beans for supper. GET OUT OF JAIL FREE. They choked

on Monopoly's lie, one swallowed marbles hoping to choke.
Where they slept, father's wife kept them, fingers folded.
Remember Europe's ghettos? Ann's diary? Neighbors
can share their bread or let cats eat you. Prisoners hurt.
Their handcuffs are real, bars minus a trial. Children
who flew from that mousey brown house? No sand

man for their dreams. Love's tin cup holds only sand.
To walk the lighthouse, its circling steps, I still choke
knowing silence is a cell without windows. I fold
this note to you, sit memory's dirt floor. Neighbors
slept at night. I kept these spoons to dig what hurts.
I saw my brothers live the life of spiders. Children

are not born to choke on sand nor lie wingless as flies
upon their bed. Hurt has its season.
Still, I will call their names *Bread* and *Wine,* ask my neighbors,
the angels, to bring them ten thousand summers.
I will speak of it now and in the time to come.

Night

You are twelve years old, early autumn, a day so warm windows,
doors stand open. Saturday, one sister washing dishes, brothers
in their bedroom, your father, stepmom passed out in bed. Home
brew. Whiskey. Their tanks, full. Your older sister pulls brush
curlers from her silky hair, teases, combs it, lots of spray. Girls
meeting tonight, Lori's house. Your sister's president of Y-teens.
You need tennis shoes, maybe someone needs a babysitter.
Money is good. Your father wakes, a grizzly poked by a stick.
Passing your brothers, he crushes a light bulb barehanded.
Because it's there. Because he can. He demands to know who didn't
empty the mop bucket. From the bathroom, your sister's head pops,
Me, she says. Her hair's done up, striped blouse pressed; it hangs
loose over her jeans. You don't know why he grabs her hair, starts
punching her face with his fist over and over, why your stepmom
decides to join the bear's dance of punch and choke. Why does
a kid keep watching such a scary movie? There's no Afghan to pull
over your head. Anyway, you think the neighbors called for help,
the cavalry's coming. Snot's running down your face and tears
and from the kitchen your sister says, *They're gonna kill her...*
She says it like *we have to do something or else.* What would that
be? You have to pee, but the bathroom's too close to those awful
sounds of hurt and hate. When the angels come, at last, and your
sister staggers down the hall bleeding, both ears, her left eye (you
didn't know an eye could bleed), an eye swollen nearly inside out,
you *feel it* and wince. Her breast's the size of a purple melon, choke
marks like rope burns circle her neck. A wet bath towel gets thrown
over your sister's face. *Clean yourself up,* your stepmom snaps.
In a living room chair, you are an earthquake, you are the epicenter
and the seismograph needle. So much blood you think your sister
will probably die. You cannot speak. Maybe you nod your head,
start to lift your hands toward the towel sliding off what's left
of your sister's face. No, you cannot. The small animal of your body
has crawled into its cave to wait for mercy, paint what has
happened on the walls.

Rain

Summer nights after our shift
Marilyn, Theresa and I sit on
the bench outside the ER.

We sip cold coffee, smoke,
watch the big dipper
refuse to burn out.

Stubborn as Sam Morgan's
stiff lungs, coughing years
of mill dust. They will not die,

but cannot live. Can this
be the same sky that bowed
to Cleopatra? tormented Van Gogh?

We are nurses, not Shamen,
we whisper what we know.
Our daughters swim faster

than this moon, our sons' faces
are passengers in train windows,
every half second, science invents

gizmos for us to memorize,
red alarms, green beeps, chants
to raise the dying. We are plain

gray doves that will fly
from this bench the way tide
leaves the shore. Others will come,

sponges to bathe the lonely,
webs to bandage the angry.
One day, we will leave

this world, overnight
we'll become the rain.

LONG DISTANCE

The woman on the phone talks with her friend. Next week:
Myrtle Beach, ten days, vacation, a visit with Ruth and Joe.
It's Thursday, garbage night, just now, dusk. The dog's asleep
dreaming on a rug. Her husband opens the kitchen door, gray

as a weathered fence, *I don't know what's wrong, but I didn't*
think I'd make it back to the house. She knows. She knows
it's not far to their drive's mouth and the carried can? Half full.
She knows right now their life's on fire, not a big flame, some-

thing electrical in the cellar, smoldering, doing its deed in
darkness. She reads his skin, a newspaper and haunting faces
rise before her, years of men/women, they walk toward her
field hands the hottest August days. Out of breath, pushing

wooden carts piled high with their good hearts, red as apples,
everywhere in her kitchen, the sweet smell of rot. How fast
can she give an aspirin, a nitro, grab her keys, load him
in her car? All the way to ER, they barely speak, but what's

twenty minutes in a lifetime? The Grand Canyon's down road.
She lifts the ER's red phone, *My husband's a cardiac patient.*
She does not know the voice spilling words like pills on
a counter. They need a plan, way to escape, but he's wired up

looks *sick* in that flowered gown. How many tests will he pass/
fail? *In my top drawer,* he worries sheets, *there's a pair*
of earrings for Summar (our daughter) *for Christmas.* She studies
the floor, tells him she has to pee. A lie. How many women

cry in bathroom stalls? She washes her face, pops a mint.
Day three, his cath shows two blockages. Widow Maker.
Two stents given. Thursday, she thought, was her day off.
She believed Ruth was on the phone, but it was God,
and when He asked for her husband, she lied.
She told God, *Sorry, he's not home.*

Everyone in the Room Is Needed:
Clinical Rotation, Labor & Delivery, 1979

I didn't know how to talk around doctors, afraid
my questions might sound dumb, I saved them
for nursing profs, or later, reviewed my notes.

To be learning so much, so fast, I was happy
for a chance at the table. Breathing the same air
as seasoned OB nurses, scrubbing our hands

in twin sinks, I thought their knowledge might
float over to my forearms, enter skin like soap.
First case, seeing my first birth, a C section,

my heart was a bluebird flying inside my chest.
A beautiful almond princess appeared, her head
a crown of soft black curls, the sweetest fruit

from her mother's belly. I cried, standing the deck's
edge. Star struck, I kept watching the strange dance
a hand-and-eye-ballet, doctors and nurses pass silence

like instruments with their eyes. Until needle count,
flawless. One needle missing, the docs can't close.
Topside, a nurse tallies sponges, shakes blood-stained

gauze, but the world stops
without the curved needle. Hearts beat, second hands
sweep over numbers, blood sloshes through our veins.

The princess goes to the nursery, but surgery cannot
proceed. On hands and knees, my pupils search, a flash-
light's beam, any shiny spine. Several moments pass.

I find their needle, a button popped off in snow. One doc
said, *Well, it wasn't a total waste of time having a student
in the room.* Without tainting the field, I struggled to stand

hand off my gem. Another class almost done.
I was working to rise from being forever on the floor.

Nurses Stand Up for Healthcare Reform

Mr. President, Speaker of the House, Senators, Congressmen,
I ask the chair to recognize the delegates standing in scrubs.

No sir, we did not fly on private jets. We car-pooled.
Yokes? Yes sir, the draped stethoscopes are symbolic.
Yes sir, we are tired. Coffee would be nice.
No sir, donuts are not necessary, but the bathrooms?
Thank you. Thank you very much.

The speaker calls on Urgent Care.

Thank you Mr. President, Mr. Speaker, Senators, Congress.
I make a motion when a guy lacerates fingers, smashes his thumb
in a hot mess machine and he's working for less
than minimum wage, driving a 1987 Lick-and-a-Promise,
barely enough money for gas,
wearing work boots that wouldn't pass for flip-flops,
apologizing to me for bleeding on sheets, and I know he has
to spend the five dollars he's got (counting change) for milk
and bread on his way home, I make a motion
he can go to the COME ON DOWN pharmacy 24/7
where someone will be kind, offer their pen,
show him the one line to print his name
let him use the drive through and honor his voucher
for antibiotics and ten pain pills.

I further move if this motion isn't drafted and passed
say it dies in some committee or has a seizure on some floor
I move that all the grunts who end up having hand surgery
(which costs 80K)
and lose the use of their dominant hands
be made wards of the state and get to live
(wife, kids, mother-in-law, dogs, cats and all)
in the governor's mansion for free.

That's it. That's all.

MERCY

This grandmother I'm holding the phone for lives on
a pension of chalk and ashes. Tonight, walking to the grocery,
a van hit her, kept going.

A man (she said he was a white man) left her, a snapped
branch in cold, honking rain. I mean lying near a storm sewer
with two broken legs isn't sitting a counter, reading

the blackboard's menu deciding what you want,
what you'll settle for if they're out of tomato bisque.
Even at dusk, there's no mistaking a woman's shape for crumbs.

Our ice bags negate piles of warm blankets. Who knew her
husband was just discharged? Heart attack. Legally blind.
They are both crying.

I love you. I'm so sorry, please take your pills, on the counter by
the toaster, yes, I will try to call Ted. I don't know. I know, don't
please, don't cry. Here, talk to the nurse, she knows.

But, I don't.
I don't know when her surgery will be or how her legs will heal.
I don't know if she'll get pneumonia or blood clots.

There's a risk. That's what I know.
I know she wears the quiet face of kindness and this room's
bloated with noise. I know this phone is black; we're at the station,

my feet ache and she needs the pain shot she won't take.
I want to believe she will get well enough to go home,
fill his pill pods, wash his back. Like me, they have a life,

a house where the roof slopes, so the rain and snow
won't come in, maybe peonies border her porch.
In my pocket, there's a scratch off ticket for long shots.
I saw a penny in her purse. That's what I know.

Forgiveness

I.

Dr. Brown wears his black wing tips, navy blue suit, After Life
cologne, his same wavy white hair. Tall as a rocket, I want to ask
him where he splashed down after cancer, but I don't.
We're in my cellar, wooden beams, cobwebs, painted block walls.
I pull and pull warm clothes from the dryer, big load of darks.
Surgeons, I shake my head, when you need one, they're never near,
but here we both stand, last load of the day. Dr. Brown appears
between pillowcases and my full-figured bras (the lace ones)
hanging from a metal line. He watches me unscrew the bulb
over our washer. Against cement, my flip flops whisper,
and like a dance partner, he follows my lead. I nearly apologize
for the workbench mess, the sprung mousetrap by the furnace.

II.

Upstairs, he seems tired. I nod him toward my husband's recliner.
I am a bit surprised when he sits. On the loveseat, I dump the
         basket.
You're all dressed up, I say, wondering if these are his burying
         clothes.
Yes, he replies, *it's my favorite suit, tie.*
The snap on my daughter's jeans burns my thumb. Our dog,
always glad for company, jumps, licks Dr.Brown's long fingers,
sniffs his crotch. *Sorry,* I cringe (half-smiling).
The way you toss and fold those towels, he praises.
I stop my work. *Why are you here?* I ask. *No golf?*
Not today, he sighs. The dog takes off with a dryer sheet; I lunge
to snatch it back. Our living room's not the place for Dr. Brown.
My husband's big wrench mounted on oak(a retirement gift
from his buddies), our kids' graduation photos, granny's Bible.

III.

That Tuesday in the OR, he begins.
When I was a student? I cut in.
Yes.
And they switched the order of your cases? (I need to be sure).
Yes.
*And you'd just told your golf-partner friends, said they'd soon see
their son in recovery, a hernia repair's like tailoring trousers?*
Yes.
*And then you walked in on the fifty-six year old lady already under
for her gall bladder, a diabetic?*
Yes.
*And you went 'Jesus Christ, somebody haul ass upstairs, talk
to those parents. Who the hell brought her down 'crazy.'*
Yes.
*After you stomped out, for five minutes, they were nearly peeing
their pants—thought they'd have to reverse the lady,
do the hernia kid first.*
No.
*Oh yeah. They were really scared. Me too. I was the only student
in the room.*
I remember.
You do?
Yes, he points to my legs, *your white hose.*
Why did the real nurses put me in your arm pit for first assist?
He shrugs, looks out the window at our trees.
Well, I didn't know a Deaver retractor from a Phillip's screwdriver.
*For almost three hours your tongue was my scalpel. You screamed
your way through layers of fat and fascia finally pulling out the rotten.*

IV.

(I put hand on hip and talk real loud for this part):
*You think I didn't know how fast you had to change your game plan?
That for one moment you looked the fool?*
He rubs and rubs his eyes, studies his hands, my bifocals.
I'm sorry, he says, *I'm really sorry.*
All the while he pets and pets our Belle.
Coffee? I offer.
Sure, he says as he wrestles stiffness to stand, *and please, show me
where the towels go.*

COLONOSCOPY:
ENCOURAGING PATIENTS TO VENT

It's just air we tell them, but many are bashful
as lilies especially middle-aged men, the ones
who still wear white briefs.

While I scoop their clothes, take their vital signs,
I'm Katie Couric asking, *how was the prep? Able*
to drink it all? Your last movement, what color was it?

If you walk in shy, you'll leave proud because we're
not talking The Price is Right; this is Survivor. The island
fills and empties with new members of the pineapple brotherhood.

You can imagine the gut's surprise, mid-December waking
a brown bear in his den. You weren't expecting a stick of dynamite
lit and thrown. And now, your body says, *Come on down,*

You're bathroom king for a day. One man felt called
to witness (I swear), he said I read three Playboys, one Smoky
Mountain knife catalog and two Reader's Digests before the muskets

slowed, and I had time to think between magazines, time to make
a plan. *Go on,* I said. Well, after I scrubbed the john, I got myself
showered and shaved. When I thought it was safe, I dressed. I nod.

I went to the cellar, took down my gun, two shells and loaded both
barrels. In the kitchen, I grabbed the plastic jug by its neck, swung
it like a duck, stood it on a backyard stump,
blasted it to Kingdom Come.

That, he said, felt like justice.

Breast Cancer Survivors:
Writing Workshop, Thursday Night at Burger King

Because we'd been locked out of the art gallery
(a sculptor forgot to leave the key she'd slipped into her purse),
I said, *Maybe we should cancel class.* (November, six women
huddled in one car, breath steaming windows like we're
cooking soup). *No, no, no.* They chant.
We've done our homework. Okay, I say, *but where?*
Someone quips, *Burger King.* We laugh. *Okay, meet me there.*

At first the corner booth reminds me of crows, back and forth
catcalls, seven kids from *I don't give a shit* high school,
skull tattoos, spike dog collars, blue hair, every phrase
laced with *fuck* and *bitch.* I'm the workshop teacher.
I am well and start to wonder if what we're watching might be
the end product of a terrible experiment. Mold bubbling up
from having it your way.

We get in line, buy our coffee. Two of the women smoke.
Class begins the old way, my tape recorder hums piano music,
ocean spray against a rocky shore, slow deep breaths.
Spiral notebooks open hymnals in our laps. And I like
how one woman gives her husband hell (roses sent first time
after her breast was removed), how another tells her kids
not to be afraid in foster care, she hopes they'll soon sleep

under one roof. And God, well, she's afternoon-turn shift
leader in a hair net dressed like somebody's Mom who'd
really be pretty if she had teeth. She's barking orders to grunts
in back and listening very carefully to the real deal,
the *No happy meals sold here* poets.

Their journal entries stab of biopsy needles, the physics
and bullshit of lugging Ensure cases up two flights
of stairs, outside apartment, winter's ice, letters to lost breasts,
shock of being bald, endless puking after chemo.

You might not believe me, but those kids in the corner booth?
They disappeared.
I don't know when, but this really happened, just ask God.

SPARED

The pretty nurse with all those initials behind her name
(almost an alphabet) is fretted up at the trauma conference.
Her power point bullets too slow for her sermon.
She says her colleagues should not get giant fries, double
whopper-bacon-cheeseburgers, mega Cokes.

They must not reward themselves after a multiple-vehicle
call (semi, three cars). After lifting a girl's head from a ditch,
a boy's arm near a tree, a pregnant woman's body mashed
through a steering wheel. After holding sheets around all that
so other freeway drivers might be spared.

After not crying or puking, not losing it (almost never,
maybe 20-30 years) she wants them to know the better path
is *exercise*. A big fireman sitting next to me sighs.
I pass him my maple cream stick. He smiles.

Trembling with conviction, she explains how we need a gym
at every hospital, (the fireman chokes, I can't look at him),
because as a flight nurse, she goes there: to bike, run,
do a thousand crunches, walk her chained bear
on the treadmill so it will sleep.

I think of my colleagues, the night they identified two
carloads of teens by their socks (with the parents).
I was not the nurse that night. I was not a mother screaming,
nodding *Yes* to socks. I was not a father walking through fire
holding a son.

The afternoon my friend's baby drowned?
I was home weeding zinnias, a meatloaf in the oven.
People say they don't know how to believe, but God is real.
I have seen the work of His hands. I have felt His mercy.

EVENING PRAYER

Our bodies which art in decline
hallowed be thy buckled floors
dusty plaster of crumbling knees.
The projector's room inside our temples
housing reels of dreams?
Blessed be its vista of colors, seascape
and pampas grass, monsters
slain by our Mothers' voices.

Blessed be this harvest
silver shocks found in our hair
sagging timbers of upper arms
the jaw's hammock.
Blessed be the parade
of brown spots giggling across
cheeks and nose. Plenty as nest eggs,

we are yoked and speckled. Bless our breasts,
some cut away like roses, the rest
napping in our bras. Bless those nipples,
all electricity passed through them
free of charge. Bless also the bladder's
sonar, twilight's tow rope leading us
to the bathroom. Blessed be warm smell

of bean soup rising from the gut's kitchen,
blessed be the rumble of those pots and pans.
And quiet barges inside our veins, tugs
returning dirty blood, valves opening
like locks? Hallowed be their red seas,
blessed be their captains. Give thanks
for once being able to run, making love

and call the ears' tiny bones home.
The foggy windows where memory stands,
small in her flannel gown, waving
to fast train of days, blowing kisses
to the moon? Blessed be this child's
blonde garland of curls
and welcome her one night
as the star she is into thy kingdom.

FROM

BOTH SHOES OFF: POEMS (2016)

VII.

Press a glass to the wall of memory's house,
for work done there was not much to look at,
no trumpet players, no violins.

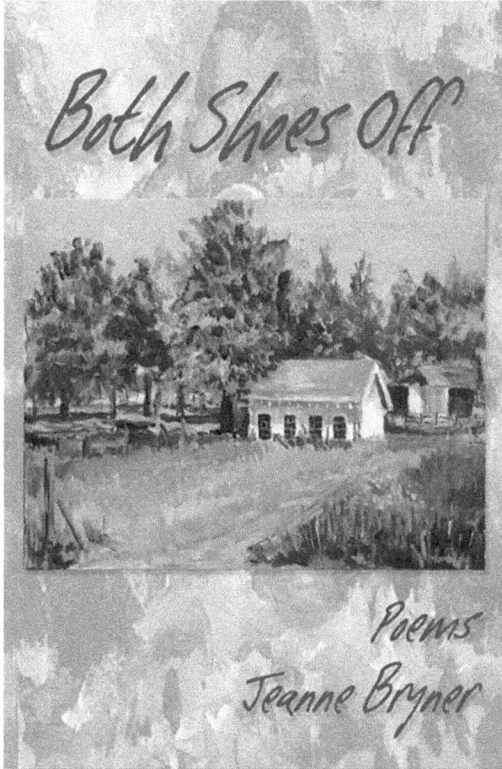

GULLS IN THE CORNFIELD

All of their wings are bruised,
and with their coats blown open
my husband says they are young boys
running home from school,
hurrying to throw down books,
grab a fist full of cookies,
gulp milk from a jug.
His eyes are worse than mine.

Far from the ocean, caught now
in hay bracken, they seem
to search for a map,
any compass to point them back.
There appears to be no captain,
 just rowdy sailors
milling about the great basin
of my neighbor's cornfield.

They pitch and swagger, screech
and scream into each other's face.
No punches land, but it makes me think
they drank last night.
Still, I have seen them in dress
whites, loved them
when they are not so manic.

I've watched them rise, fan out
a lace tablecloth blowing easy on a line.
Without partners, they have learned to waltz.
Against a blackboard of winter trees,
bodies take the shape of letters,
a lonely, crazy alphabet—
a language only the homeless know.

Mom, please send socks.
Dad, did you find me a transmission?
What? You want to date other guys?

The mail's so slow, they just keep writing.
A great mystery, their suspension, mid-air,
how we both landed next to barns and calves
far from any warm sea breeze, salty taste of waves
no wonder they cry.

The Oxen

We went to our wagon, two orphans
reaching for the nuns, starved for sweetness
born again in those covers where we slept
closer than spoons in a drawer,
our backs turned away from knives.

Still, we bought a saw, stacks of wood, stuff
to fix walls. And how many board feet
of maple, pine, oak did I catch
on the backside of its teeth?

Shavings dancing like fireflies in our hair
incense of heart wood lulling us careless
making us unafraid. But, able blades
(more than once) caught us both.

Fifty years? Hulls of empty bandage boxes
blood puddles leading upstairs. The blue plates
we threw at each other? The ones stamped.
I don't love you anymore?
We swept them up, buried them on the trail.

Soft gauze bound our eyes, hands-to-shoulders
we staggered through coiled dark. In pairs
good doctors arrive; bring pills to mend our parts.
My apron fades, we read our books
drift off before the mystery ends.

WATCHING MY NEIGHBOR IN HIS FIELDS

All the long morning, T-shirts get
blessed with sweat. My farmer
neighbor grooms his rustling grass.
Below hay mist, yellow confetti puffs,

the tractor pulls, August heat drags him.
He holds on. A test of wills forcing hay
to pack/leave; grass knows it has a place.
Dusk, he leans against fence rails,

fingers laced, chews a weed like a straw.
Evening air, bunnies run over his body;
it lies yonder under the tractor's thrum.
And he's thrown his son into summer—

the deep blue end of its days, taught him
the ballet of its scissors and combs.
Looking forward, looking back, he cuts,
binds and loads. One eye on his mirror,

the other on the sky. Swim or sink
play is done; guys learn to work—the boy
grabs and throws and stacks.
The price of milk's down; his sheds

are on their knees, still, he brings us sweet
corn, plows our driveway for free. I shake
my head. Later, when calves get watered,
get fed, without a fuss, the farmer's son

swings himself to the tractor's seat,
tines pass over the fields easy as a broom.
He hums and whistles as he sweeps
his father's floor. For almost nothing,
he cleans the church.

Why It Happens

I sit down on my blue glider to read Hemingway as my neighbor, Susan, makes her fifth pass in the wheat field. Her combine's a chariot and she's a goddess, long yellow hair French braided down her back. She drives this giant machine the way guys named Stitch and Blade ram Harleys. If she knew I was here, sipping iced tea by my barrel's red geraniums, she'd wave.

She seems dressed like a waitress at Joe's lunch counter, as well she might be, coming from a steamy kitchen to take another order for fries, BLTs. In the window cab of the green machine, she holds her toddler daughter, Jenny, on her lap. Thrust and thrum of vibrating earth and gnawing grain shimmies through their warm thighs. What is it they share in this hazy space? Row after row of sunlight, riding the dinosaur's growling neck, do they sing above its grinding smell of grease? Does the child learn the many gears of silence?

Because I'm selfish, I moved to the country. I love the bouquet fragrance of new mown hay and watching lazy dirt trail farm tractors. I enjoy this without rising early for the fields. I can witness this without ordering spring seed and fretting over rainfall and hail storms. Clouds are white elephants to me. I work where air conditioners keep my mascara lines straight.

And when calving time comes, Susan invites us to their barn. I take my daughter to see stalls convulse: blood and placentas and bawling. I explain biology cycles, birth and why it happens like it does, why it looks so messy. All the while, Susan holds Jenny astraddle her left hip, black rubber boots half stuck to straw, a dim light shines on their golden hair. Susan chews a piece of Juicy Fruit; Jenny smiles, sleepy on her mother's shoulder. They're not listening to me dwell on the delivery. The calf has started to get up: glistening, buckling, wet with his life.

Blue Mason Jar

At the flea market my husband asks
Why'd you pick it up? He's right, of course,
when he reminds me it holds no sailor's ship
but just now, cradled in your palms,
a piece of August light caught inside.

You saw your uncles on Papaw's tractor
bare chested, young and tan. Granny helps
you fix high noon's ice water.
Like a pony you gallop toward all of them

both your hands full. They smile, call you *honey*,
say *please be careful*, then *thank you*
for a chance to rest,
a pause carried to them in clean blue jars.

Soon, they will cross the crick, mow the steep
pasture, their tractor on a slant.
Even now, you don't know why
but you are afraid.

Breach Calf

The calf's hind feet point to barn rafters.
Inside his mama, he dreams a baby brother,
how they sit the moon's lap for a story.
Climbing down, he does a somersault, lands wrong.
And now this farmer, his gloved arm pushes him
back and back and back, his mama strains at her plow.
Then, other rough men, special chains, metal wrapped
just below his knees, not wanting a cripple,
a calf who cannot run or play. Mama's fresh blood,
pain's awful hands squeeze, no breath for his whistle.
The beautiful boy asleep in clean straw,
but all in the manger are still,
save his bawling mother
washing her son, calling his name to the moon.

LOCUST SHELL

Hanging sheets on the line, you find
a locust shell. It clings to a pole's breast
one of two crosses your husband cut
nailed and set some forty years ago.

Clean taste of clothespins in your mouth
and March winds, poles brace themselves
lean in, lean a little closer to the ground.
Suddenly, this dry well, a body outlined

in brown calls your hand to its brow.
What makes a woman take off alone,
no note, no time to grab her coat?
In your palm, a tiny piano with no song.

Gently, gently you elevate her shed
the cave that held her heart.
Pressed against your chest, a cupped hand
tends the husk. What fences do you pledge

allegiance to? What flag, this country?
Above sheets and towels, songbirds cast
their spell, the sky's metal blue lowers
its faraway swing set. Listen, hear again

the children's voices, years, yards
of happiness blown from wands,
even their cries from skinned knees.
Remember, forever, the brief nature of light.
With a kiss you'd heal the world.

Homeroom Poet-Mom: For the Second Graders, Catholic Elementary 1989

I did it because Sister Marilyn said I could,
because we both saw
the blindness of Pac Man
the quiet lesson of eating others
who don't look like us.

I did it because after we learn the letters
someday, somebody writes F on our paper.
Because when they don't get our pink trees
with blue apples, they point and giggle.
Mom, you hung my Mayflower upside down.

For voice I did it, because one day
they'd be called upon to right world mistakes.
I did it because the magic sweet potato
rooting its vine in water
was a Band-Aid on childhood's sinking ship,

and by the time we see the iceberg,
well, you know the rest. I did it because
Stephanie's mom *has hair like brown shoelaces,*
Kevin's grandpa's kiss *tastes like a popsicle,*
and when Brandy's dad hugs her *I feel*

like I'm flying. I did it so when the big grid fails,
the power's out, they'd be able to find the way
to their own cupboards, feed themselves and others
with whatever wheat's in the pantry. I did it because
not everybody lives at Ozzie and Harriet's, and

(at least in second grade) policemen can *be our friends.*
I did it because we are all paper dolls;
terrible and wonderful hands bend us
then throw us away. I did it because
that's my daughter chewing her pencil in row three

and in a creek, my feet sink.
As an act of contrition, I did it
for all the sins of my life.

THE GARDEN IN WINTER

Row upon row, snow waves
cover our garden.
In stiff trousers
the maple's shadow
walks his old dog.

Faint smell of pipe tobacco
drifts behind them.
From his left pocket.
the man lifts a boy

like a timepiece, engraved,
something rare and precious.
A leaf's hand pressed in stone.
Shoveling nine steps,
I watch the puppet show.

With great effort, a twisted
branch gets thrown;
the lab makes a clumsy plunge.
In cold white sand
the boy runs, then whistles
to his friend.

Come back, come back
you're out too far;
(my toy heart lunges, gulps)
and I'm too winded to swim.

VIOLETS

Across our living room they greet
each other, wave slight arms.
Good women, these neighbors
who seldom visit, never carry tales.

Sunday afternoon, buttoned
sleeves rolled up, green blouses
pressed, long gray hair
twisted back, pinned in buns.

These Pentecostal sisters come
together, bring bouquets, their
small fists full of purple flowers,
married heads bowed down.

This morning, one of their
young sisters passed. Today,
they will not be baptized in light
nor will they speak in tongues.

Both Shoes Off

You can barely remember it now.

Your mother holds a ball of yarn
passes its end to your fingers,
but where do girls go
pulling a pink clothesline?

You were thirsty.

Shimmering in the haze,
a guy with blue eyes, glasses.
His lips on your mouth
became a mountain stream.

You were someone else.

A woman lifting her daughter
from a highchair, a wife
hurrying to finish the lawn,
a new nurse giving shots.

You were happy there.

Being a mom, wiping cracker
mess in a dishcloth, smelling apples,
fresh sheets, letting go of your days
breadcrumbs thrown in the grass.

What was it like?

He was your song, your rainbow
parachute opening the thousandth time
your head to his warm shoulder
dancing in the yellow kitchen
slowly, with both shoes off.

KILLDEER

Tan river stones edge our small yellow house,
inches from the driveway, four speckled eggs.
Before she gave into the nest—fierce debates
came daily. It was both-arms-up-revival-preacher-passion
first the female, then the male, then both.

Warmer days, you lock screens, don't plan
to eavesdrop, but things happen, a breeze carries
voices in. I mean homesteading in stones? Only two
for such a risky crater? So many rocks to be rolled back,
it's work to rake ground, their antsy feet, their legs

thin as wires, but tough enough to clear a lot,
create a spot for temporary housing. Well into night
there was much discussion about traffic patterns—
my tan car, the mailman's van, our red truck—
tires scatter gravel; pass too close to this new cottage.

She screams at him, *What were you thinking?*
Our babies will never make it from here to the fields.
In a huff, she turns around. He struts toward her.
Did you see the neighbor's combine? he shouts back.
The female drags her left wing like it's breaking,

wrings her hands, and cries. Their parent eyes pierce, beep
a radar fixed on us, and they seem to never sleep,
these two spitfires whose mission is fly, feed, fret.
They watch my husband sharpen his mower's blade,
see me hang baskets of blood red begonias, bury vines,

smell smoke from fall leaves. Tomorrow, we'll lower
the porch swing, wash winter off her wrinkled face,
fetch floral glider cushions from our cellar,
but not in a rush, not in a hurry. Our fifty-third year;
slowly, slow we welcome summer as our guest.

The killdeer? They are newlyweds fussing
about paint colors, who tracked mud on the rug.
And the children who'll run next across this lawn?
They are not our worry.

DUSK

Late May and behind our houses
a road lies. The gravel suffers
a patch of skin altered by its rash,
scarred spine, years of combined ruts.
Aging fence lines pasture windswept grass.
Retired die setter, my husband's
the patron saint of teacup roses and dirt.

Dusk and our farmer neighbor slows
his tractor, over its drone he talks and listens
(two hundred acres scream his name).
My husband leans on a gray fender, his
bent fingers laced (twice in one week
he's planted peppers, tomatoes, beans).
A late frost came, now they speak
the lysis of hurts, balm to quiet them.

My husband's heart stents (all four) pale,
spent, never miss their wet tunnel's shift.
Richard's sixty cows bawling in stalls,
beg to be milked. Field mice,
the big barn, drifting voices of men,
their words the murmur of bees inside the hive,
a hammer's long sigh between nails.

GLORY

A pink sky cradles our woods tonight
October's trees become stained glass.
A restless river, this sky, though
you won't see John baptizing Jesus.

Across the soybean's center field,
daylight rolls itself up, a parlor blind
its hinge failing, a film shot
in robin egg blue, slate gray patches,

ashes to be shoveled from a grate.
And I think God is tired of walking
west, big bare feet fanning His robe.
He pauses every third step to kiss

shaky hands of leaves. Snow's being
spit, sweet, dreamy flakes circle the calves'
pen then, run away. Just now, lit
by a dying sun, twin silos rise

like church spires. A hymnal's closing,
the broken fence, evening's gentle *Hallelujah*.

Barns Painted With Quilt Squares

On country roads or near busy freeways
they surprise us, wide gray shoulders,
barns brought to life, aging church women
given an autumn corsage, bright orange-yellow-
blue-red-greens rest on their bosoms.

Wanting to honor her mother's life and art,
my friend, a woman, started this painting.
Her mother's a *master quilter*. She sees
bolts of cloth the way Leonardo saw marble.
Her scissors free squares of gingham,
triangles of feed sack, strips of calico.

Like evening porch talk, patches get sewn together.
To quilt, you must sit still, be responsible
for color choices. You will prick your fingers,
bleed, create a mess. All of this falls into your lap,
well, sometimes you think it's just too much.

The figuring out part never ends, after those squares
join hands, there's the batting and making do
for the quilt's back. Folded up in your dresser's
bottom drawer, years of scraps wave their arms.
Why not me? They seem to beg. It amazes you
fitting rows together, the simple grace of a choir.

How old hymns raise your eyes to blue sky
like those barns and their lone star postage stamps,
these love letters you keep writing to your mother.

IN VELVET:
NEW POEMS

VIII.

*We cannot hear the tanks
or know the hour they will come.*

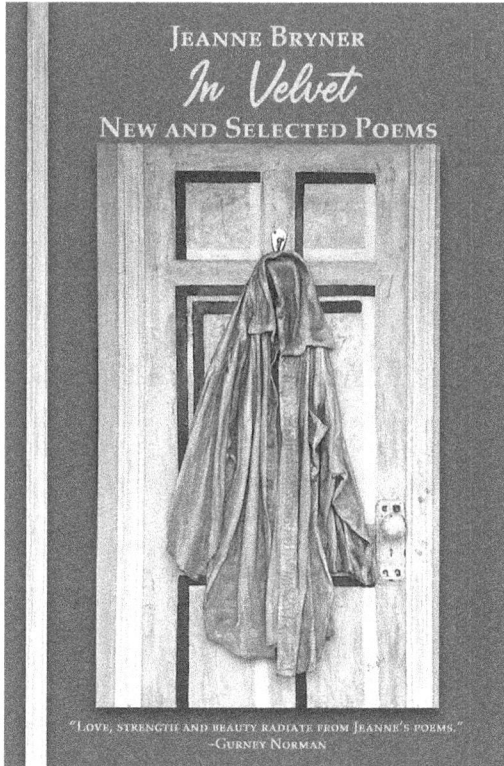

TREE

Gales, what's ahead for her, for us.
We call an arborist, a doctor for trees
who himself has a *family emergency*.

I am a messenger, not a prophet, this story's
not the tale of Shishmaref, Alaska's melting
island, its ten houses swallowed by the sea

or how a committee of suits pitch-forked
the flow of Chicago's river,
sent sewage to the Mississippi. I am one

as I hum to our tree when gathering my zinnias.
We are on a list, our number's written down.
To my eyes, the canopy is full, green, lush.

Her south limb bears some trouble, dark cracks
fissures widen, a fret, a worry. Scarred arms
stretch above the road so there's urgency.

They'll need to use the lift bucket, auger
a hole, check for softness of rot. Days
I walk the yard, I pause, stroke her blind face.

I know, I know. It's not your fault.
If she can be saved, we want it done.
We'll not ask for a Dorcas miracle, just mercy

for our friend. Without our tree, this home ends
broiled in hell's sun. No wreath shall sign
her spot, no cross name her goodness.

These eighty summers, winters all
years of bounty, years of none
Lady of Autumn, to my knees, I fall.

Frost's Farm, 1994

We rode to New Hampshire's rocky meadows,

found his home in sweet grass, plain

as a birch tree's branch, light as snowflakes

on a country lawyer's suit, longer

than wide, quiet and white. You wouldn't guess

a giant slept inside.

Approaching his porch, chin up, arms raised

I ascended the steps as if they led

to Egypt's pyramids,

grass blades bent under my feet

walking to the frog pond:

might I be changed into a sonnet?

my family to a sestina?

Frost's children had no set bedtimes,

he hid coins in the hayloft.

Hours, days, searching piles of dried

clover and always, the ground's hunger.

His pen scored stone loaves

grief the grout mending his walls

home burial, the next iambic line.

Emily's Bedroom

She wrote her letters to the world
A surgeon—her pen—
Suture to close each wound.
I have been here before—

Dollhouse set with bed
Nightstand, chair—Van Gogh's cell
His thick paints, ointment spread
Stars bandage a bruised canvas.

She did not sleep as we do—or rest
Eyes that sawed the branches bare.
She pried Truth's coffin open
In her pocket, each loved pressed.

Oh Sister, have we just one birth
To bloom sanguine and not return?
Our days worn like a sweater,
Then forgotten in a drawer?

She laughs with Austin in the sled
Moves in the dew as fog, white
Dresses wed to lavender, Vinnie
Brings her tea, sets her table
Polished silver—years of hours free.

She lanced dark nights—one, two, three
Four—loaded words by the door,
Carved her bullets by candle's light—
In her bed—no body slept.

A Hind's Daughter

Sir James Guthrie, 1883, oil on canvas

In a land scraped by wind
the lass stands alone,
seven or eight, no halo
of light, small for her age.

An oak touches her waist
leaves palm her lower back.

Her left hand chokes a cord
bound to its cabbage head.
Her right hand squeezes its knife
the blade glows, gathers heat rings
in morning sun. The quick slash
of cutting? Clearly, she's the one.

Despite absence of birthing sign,
a line reels us to her core,
her tan skirt a shadow above
the garden's wild spiraling arms.
Our black-haired girl pauses chores;
her tied bow wilts below a fixed jaw.
Like tulips, her breasts bud, ache
to flower, her shoes fused to mud.

She's no fairy, this girl with cocoa
skin, limbs russet as trench graves.
A man we cannot see—sketches,
paints her across centuries, no law
against it—the girl's stare pierces
the trail ahead—crusty dirt floors
palm a sunken bed, chair legs bear
down—outside, pigs jockey a trough.

Yes.
Her whole body knows
—already, she's there—
under thatch, under a man
his hands shelling her life.

Patches From a Family Quilt

Someone's had a breakdown, the mom.
Brain sickness is not like the movies,
though lines must be learned fast.
Manic's a sprint, sadness a jog,
electroshock therapy's no two room
schoolhouse. Psych docs aren't dad's
friends, boys from the ridge who rose
early to start teacher's coal stove.

No face book in the 50's. No,
a handshake was a sign of faith.
Who can spell what's in Mom's forest
name the witch who makes her cry?
Only she sees her same lane
in the small house, miles and miles
she follows its breadcrumbs
her rag hands wringing.

What is it when a man runs out
of family and there's a baby?
Kids get packed up, parceled out, grands
get pallets ready. Marathon of days
weeks, months. I was six weeks old,
motherless, father asked best friends
Could they take a baby?

Aunt Merle was not young
her boys both done with the Navy,
married, grown. Uncle Carl found the crib.
This was before automatic washers, throw
away diapers. I don't know how soon
I settled in, if I had colic missing Mom's
breasts. Circling Saturn, earth
and moon, Mom scuffed her floors.

Deep in pink blankets, I yawned, slept.
Aunt Merle's hands powdering me
after a bath, fixing nipples to my mouth
rocking, humming, rugs to be swept,
bread to be baked. Novel pages turn,
booties, high top shoes. Almost gone
my first three years.

Through her black hole, Mom crawled.
I was weaned, potty trained
had my own best friend. Uncle Carl
busy building us a new house.
On Lane Street, they came for me
had my sisters in their Nash.

It was before car seats, and I threw
my backseat fit. Lost, I flew
inside that space, wren against glass,
sweet faces I knew melting
under gentle shade of their ash.

ABOVE ALL

I am driving to join my friend.
Nurses, we've spent years tending bodies.
Her son's wife died: two babies, motherless,
are learning to breathe inside the hull
of that house.
She's minding the children, her love
(this is the only way to say it)
is a bonfire beside their tent.

Traveling in morning darkness,
sun pours, but I'm cold. Twelve hours
to arrive, share a week with her while
her son's job flies him away.
I am weaving my car through Cincinnati,
crossing the river, soon the bridge
will be gone, mountains come close.

I had a friend who thought he'd sleep
every other night as a boy, have more time
to fish with his dad. When we're young
a billion stars, coins, fountains, endless wishes.

We think striking a deal is same as a match,
every loss, chalk to blackboard, teaches us
how tight to hug fathers when they leave.

ASSISTED LIVING

Beside his chair walks a shadow,
but where's the candle to lift, to light?
What patron saint protects him?
Our town's wheelchair man, his legs
bent and angled—crooked feet shod.

Long ago, he knew the forge. See—
leather gloves with fingers cut away?
Twice a day he slogs himself to town,
then back. They say he must,
or off he goes to fetid wards,
a boy denied warm mush.

Lime vest tied, pigeon thin, he leaves/
returns to his window's sill. Ukraine's
flag hooked to his pole. Still, a van
hit him; tired clay, over he fell
upon the road's wilderness of us—
a moving forest of trunks and knees.

He buys coffee—ten guys adrift,
tethered to our halfway house. *It's hell.*
they snarl, *our rooms are pens.* From
their smoky circle, our sage rises
pale as a fallen moon, growing smaller,
his arms and face pocked. We can't tell

if he remembers July's sweet lake.
Feet on the soggy dock, mother waves,
noon they taught him to swim. *Just
lie back and float, Buddy; I'm here,
I am right here.* In his father's hands,
his whole body.

HONEY

It was winter: he needed his overcoat
the heavy one, longer than the plaid he wore
for hunting. We're shadows, the living room
near the door he busted down, repaired.
Mom wouldn't let him in—he was drunk
and hit her when he was that way. To be cursed
slapped, choked, used like a mop pushed rough
against floors, cold slab to shoulders, hips
a woman becomes a rag. But this time
he was hurt, a car accident, he was drunk with
a rack of broken ribs taped round and round
for stability so he might heal, go back to work.
Each breath, a fist, a knife to cough, a noose
to take a drag off his cigs. He'd buttoned
his shirt, combed his black hair, feet stuffed
into his boots. I was six or seven.
He had a waiting chair to sit—doctor,
lawyer or courthouse. His cracked ribs scream-
ing, lungs aflame under the tape, his wreck's mess.
I was the lone kid in morning's room.
He was sober, leaned sideways, edged low, hug-
ging himself like when a woman's water breaks,
bloody show, labor's early knot of struggle
a strain to do any scene of daily living:
put on a coat, seek aid, take cover.
Not a fence, but a fire he was passing through
this pain across his mid-section, wide white
tape squeezing under his coat's gray wool
somewhere, a sheep shorn, castrated, now
a sort of cape draped over his right shoulder.
My father asked, no, he begged me, his baby
daughter, to help thread his fist inside the coat's
silky sleeve of darkness. Violets dot my night-
gown as I stood barefoot, ballerina tiptoes,
fixed the grizzly's paw into his great coat.
Thank you honey, he said—his voice strained,
hushed—sweet word he called me just this once.

171

Call From West Virginia to Ohio, 1956

We look hard for the broken toy, the rock we
called home plate. Mother's alive there, so we look,
watch her able hands shove the belly of her washer. Hard
as it is, a baby inside, one on her hip. She feeds diapers for-
ever through mangle rollers, drops them in her basket. The
morning's work starts in darkness. Her man's breath, his promise broken.
Smell of bacon grease and bleach, her lips red as a toy
doll. Neighbor girls, more beautiful than their horses, circle the
block, cowgirl boots, red-blonde hair. Purdy's boy coughs his rock.
Burr's Grocery is close, open every day, but we
are too small to go alone, diapers, I can fold. Granny called
today, Mother's laugh danced through our house. News from home
is wind chasing the wolf away. It is ham on our plate.

WOMEN IN THE KITCHEN

We are talking about our grown children
in her kitchen as she scalds cabbage leaves.
Pink meat, its spices wait in her bowl.
I envy the dance of her hands, quick polka

steps and sweet echo of her mom's voice
when she laughs. In our old jeans and Saturday
shirts we're not Thelma and Louise, though
we shot our red convertible across the canyon

of seventy years. She's making meals to freeze.
Her sister's lady-parts have thrown in the towel,
surgery will slow her, sit her down for weeks,
but family's hunger? The bear who never sleeps.

So much warmth in my best friend's home
our words are lemon birds in thistle
sentences sprinkle seeds in the forest
of truth and trouble.

Women, an aproned pair
pulling our cart under the waning moon
of a gypsy life, lost in steam and fog. We
don't see the artist, but a painting blooms.

Boiled, the leaves vein a lovely green;
naked, the meat's skin softens to brown.

We braid blades of high grass
her grandson's heart surgery, summer
gardens, her back pain and MRI. Bodies
of cabbage rolls get stacked and stacked
the oven's aglow.

We're both inside this canvas
where the meat and leaves are buddies
snoring in a foxhole and cannot hear the tanks
or know the hour they will come.

DRIVING THROUGH AMISH COUNTRY
FIRST SUNDAY, FAMILY DAY AT THE DRUG REHAB

My husband says, *I can't go with you; we can't fix*
this curse. I straighten a rag rug on my kitchen floor,
grab my purse and keys. Our daughter's dog bears witness
to my *God help us* voice. *Her heart will break*
if your arms don't catch her. He quips, *she has a sponsor.*
Love is a whip; my hopes for his hand vanish in smoke.

It's summer, Amish families walk home from church, no smoke
rises above their chimneys. Craftsman, bonnets, come together, fix
barns, slice apples for pies. I bet there's no dog hair on their floors.
Gawkers pull over, idle cars, watch work horses plow, witness
the old ways, grooming the land, mindful, careful not to break
its spine with tractor weight. Sonny, our cousin, was a sponsor.

At Sonny's wake, a sobbing man grabbed his cold palm. His sponsor—
Sonny—gone. Grief buckled the man's knees. Sonny smoked.
Cancer ate him. Doctors used their big book, still, no drug to fix
his cells. Brother to my husband's heart, Dave recalled a floor
of Sonny's home where they'd wrestled as boys, witnessed
Superman on TV, stirred a bit of trouble by breaking

a clay nativity. Aunt Ruby wept, forgave them, *Nice things break*
boys. You said you're sorry; help me gather the pieces. Sponsors
are ladders, will patch a roof in an ice storm. Folks must divorce smoky
bars, friends who frequent them. The fresh path? No easy fix
no spray to erase Honky Tonk smells, gritty cornmeal floors.
Couples ache to slow dance, bands need to play. Witness

faded jeans, worn boots, country music weekend singers. Witness
how we know all the words to Patsy's "*Crazy.*" It breaks
the Top Ten Truth charts to hear them, and where's the sponsor
to drive us home? We throw the dice, someone's life is smoke.
Both our kids made poor choices, knots a parent can't fix.
It keeps a mother up at night, journaling, walking her floors.

Court days we saw our kids in jumpsuits/handcuffs? The floor
barely braced our feet. A crusty judge, we had to witness
their names called. A spear went through our eyes. No break
for tears, wooden chair room, strangers stare, no sponsor
steadied our gait. Gunnysacks covered our heads, we were smoke
trailing the ash of our children's plague. Us? No kind fix.

In group, I circle-sat inches from a son, witnessed him break his mom.
I wish you'd die. His tongue's bullet, she fell to the floor, eyes dilated, fixed
fingers clutched a gold cross. No sponsor. Our room filled with smoke.

WHY WE MUST HELP UKRAINE:
DOCUMENTARY, RUSSIA INVADES AFGHANISTAN, 1979

The camera lingers, a voice compares
Russia's invasion to America's concerns
with Vietnam, super powers
against farmers and nomads.

A woman who is no longer young, thick
across her middle tells of being a mole
living in tunnels. Weeks without privies
her body's putrid smell.

Balding, a Russian officer sits his oak
study, leather chair, points to his chest
where Russian soldiers strapped grenades
so *if things went badly* (captured by Muslims)
they'd not be tortured.

Last to be interviewed —
a young boy, maybe ten years old.
Squatted down, he stares into a campfire
speaks slowly, slow.

They came into our house, shot my father here
he points to his left shoulder
and here (two times, he pats his chest).

His fist rubs and rubs the green
of his shirt.
Then, they shot him in his head.
He pauses there

hard to watch the movie again — in color
knowing already how it ends —
and no mute button for the sounds

the writhing noises a man makes
dying in front of his family.

Then my brother jumped from his bed
started hitting the soldiers who shot our father.
Two of them held my brother, a third cut
his fingers off with a bayonet,
he was helpless then. . . .

                The boy starts to cry,
looks from the interpreter
to the camera man recording his story.

 Then, the soldiers beat my brother.
His hands were bleeding; he was screaming.
One soldier stuck his rifle in my brother's ear
                a bullet came out
the other side of his head.
He fell dead beside our father.

The camera man turns to wretch,
the brave boy hugs his chest, rocks
on haunches, counts again, cold
twitching digits on his mother's floor.

            He is old, he is ancient
this holy man wiping red eyes
on his prayer cloth, sleeves
of his green cotton shirt.

IN VELVET

Gaza. A glazed woman pets her son.
He lies limp, bloody; another Mozart
crushed. We cover eyes, ears, mouth.

Let me call him back, the young buck
his horns in velvet. Yes, call him back,
legs splayed, a country road, my daughter
in ponytails, aglow, wild to see him.

Early fall, my sister "Granger of the Year"
Tuesday, small town Appalachia.
They'd asked me to speak. Yes, call Sara
back, smiling in her shirtwaist dress,
surprised by the wood plaque bearing
her name, neighbors, friends clapping.

I call the wide cake back, its sweet roses
Aunt Merle dipping red punch, neat
rows of plastic forks, the pink napkins.
Sara's husband kisses her cheek; her baby
girl soon to be homecoming queen
not one tumor seed stirs in her calf.

These, the days of sun's abundance
months before any shedding
velvet grows fast, fast, feeds the child
nuzzling meadow gardens, full
of blood's breast milk, the thirsty
horns nurse, the antlers harden.

I want us to spend our lives inside
that thick castle room, grow old
in gray folding chairs. Go ahead,
axe my hands instead of theirs.
For more time in that light, I will
paint trees with my toes. Listen,

I want to join the grange, learn
their secret handshake. See me
now, paper lost, pencils broken
both palms open. See how
the icing stiffens and for the yearling
hunting season comes.

Bargaining at My Husband's Bedside: Coronary Step Down Unit, 2002

"So we move another summer closer
to our last summer together — "
—Linda Pastan

Your groin's bruise is purple like mother's iris.
They bloom in June just for your birthday,
she lied to the girl I was.

The fair's gone; we can't be eighteen again.
There's a bell to ring, but no sledge
for your pale hands. Past ten, timid doctors
round, miss sleepy bullets of family queries.

Rooms smelling of brine await us all and
wheelchairs stained with mud. A door thuds,
curtains slide, we become the machines'
blank-eyed stare
taste IV salt, fear rising like gall.

I love night's nurses best, how they wear
blankets like shawls. Coffee not sleep,
I count beeps, floor tiles, dots of cars
inching out and in hospital lots.
Headlights twirl, wink like fireflies.

Jeeps, sedans, SUVs creep along,
like you and me, find their place in line.
In here, outside, there's no rest. Folks
just drive. They go away, circle blocks,
red eyes skimming, every breath erased
sealed under glass. You are the lion

I am not. I trembled when death
buried his face in my hair.
Let's make a deal . . .
Last night, he whispered, stroked my neck
On your back, what's one more scar?

Now, who's afraid to sit down, fall asleep?
Come morning, I will ask the old nun
wheezing, wringing her prayer cloth
pacing room-to-room
what yarn was spun—before and after—
I let his tongue enter my mouth.

Letter from the Trenches

Winter's early yard, birds consume crabapple berries.
The ornamental pear won't survive—rain. I'm afraid
too much bog, mold and sodden ground brings root rot.

Our cousin, father of two, thinks she'll pull through.
Wait, he says, *see what happens next spring*.
Sonny wrestles a mess of tumors, lung cancer.

Him leaning close to brown trouble, palpating vein and leaf,
studying our tree while he's being sawed in half—well, hell,
his words hold pure fire. Morning fog and dampness swell

gray steam from coffee. We're the curb's sad mattress, tan stain
and sick bed smell. If not for our dog we'd loaf till noon.
Out of breath, out of good ideas like maintaining calm

not scream as the noose tightens, but fight hard as Sonny.
Most nights, asleep, I dream I'm scolding my husband
Do not forget your heart pills. Medicine for him,

Sonny, us? It's a grapevine over a gorge, keeps us swinging
pill after pill. My mind spins. I make plans, write stuff down,
know wind chimes won't sound the alarm, our dog almost

never barks and those chutes scattered in the dale?
Their clan's already here.

BEGIN IN LOVE

My cousin still cries when Beth dies in *Little Women*.
Uncle Bud's girl, at sixty, needed heart surgery.
We all drove, sat while her husband stripped bark
from his hands, such a whale hospital, where sun
pounds and pounds against windows. Beached

there, a land-locked town of crazy lanes, hot tar
where nobody waves you in, and above us,
a glass bridge, a marvel, a fancy plank. Below
you can't count the street people waving signs,

ragged faces of war, HUNGRY, begging coins.
Comrades, their keen eyes shiv your flank
when you pass. They drive rusty carts aft/ahead.
My cousin? The clean axe finds its trunk,

they've split her chest. And in this scarred room?
Whispers knit the white space; it's a bandage
we roll and wind as we wait. Her husband's
mustache brushed flat, fake coffee we sugar

and stir. Uncle Bud inched through Normandy
so how they saw and seam her—bloody gloves,
scalpel to flesh, nurses sopping the mess—is a wound, no
grenade. Come lunch, we spoon salty soup, salad, bread.

Amid vapors, masks down, two surgeons arise.
Brown nurses come, sing the song of dreads, then
bend to their work, hands-to-drum. Pat kisses her hand,
traces her brows, her cheek—good wife, best friend.

The place she floats, we circle. Her body's changed,
wrapped in sheets, lavender, pale, asleep. Washed from
foamy tides, caught in a net of plastic ropes, she's our pearl
her strange bed so like a boat we must pull and pull to shore.

Day the Ladle's Handle Broke

Ellwood Engineered Castings has identified the employee killed when a malfunction caused molten steel to be poured over him.
> —*Tribune Chronicle*, January 17, 2024
> Trumbull County, OH

Now their names drift, atoms floating across space
day the ladle broke, baptized three men, red
liquid fire. *It was the 50's,* the old doctor said,
I was ER green when they came—melted flesh

coveralls, gloves, morphine, morphine. Their wives
arrived, one pregnant, one in pin curls, the last
fell, writhing to the floor, blue slippers lost.
I will long recall blade of his shale knife,

horror's story, scalded men, burnt hair smell,
screams, twisted faces, his wallet's card for life.
Hushed fathers never spoke names of those men
carried thermoses, pails, coats out the door.

That night—one drank the coffee, one ate the Spam
the blind one fell, writhing to the floor.

Blessed is the Heart

Peacemaker inside the great barn
father of us all, he passes the meat
plate, its thick roast to the left
his fork last in line.

Bless his bulbous nose, ruddy face
and bloodshot eyes, his slur of words
over time. This living space offers
no remote, not one easy chair.

The smallest guy in the loft
and blind, he works every crimson shift.
The mine field's chaplain
he lifts the wounded, no job

shuffling in the abbey. No monastic
bells, he gets us up, keeps us going.
Rises after our staggering falls
as though nothing's happened.

*There's a time to be sick
and a time to be well.* Vespers
then tamp the sludge and straw.
Strain and both his temples throb

mercy given again and again
as he hurls himself over the bombs.

BLUE SHIRT

I had a blue shirt, the kind you throw
over a blouse for evening's chill.
Our house had veined ankles, swollen
knuckles, friable sashes. We knew
enough to know the walls
held no pink fluff.

Hunting fields of flea markets
crusty garage sales, we wasted days.
Piles of stuff get thrown aside
shirts and purses hang together
no strong backs or loose change
to fill them. Like blown scarves

we moved inside close winds,
so please don't say I must not
grieve my shirt's passing. Its good will
collar, its frayed cuffs, buttons still
sewn tight. Three best dollars
I ever spent.

My bike had a baby seat, a strap
kept my daughter safe. My knees
moved, my hands held metal bars.
Unbuttoned, the shirt billowed
a cape in the wind. Weightless,
we touched the moon, flew back.

No compass, some juice, gravel
and sweat. Miles of dirt roads, hay
smells, small arms laced my flank.
Her chest became the warm rice pack
to my spine. When she gave way
to sleep, her cheek and wee heart

pressed the soft grain
sky blue corduroy waves.

                                   Heaven.
Sometimes, you get so close.

Midden

To not gesticulate or fuss
about the weight
of wet sofa cushions
moonlight's apneic snoring.

To not question banishment
refrigerator hinges
begging doors
a holey sock, catatonic
from losing her mate.

To not grumble
about overcrowding
your smelly neighbors
piled on mattresses
of moldy bread.

To find meaningful content
decaying on hillsides
couplets of soup cans
running over
one verse into another.

To consider being dumped
as traveling to a faraway place
a blue satellite lands
on the bright planet
of empty ketchup bottles.

To not curse the squish
of half-rotted peaches
to embrace the harmony
of leftover chicken bones.

To let the sun's kiss
bring comfort to legions
of one-eyed teddy bears
legless kitchen chairs.

To approach the end
smiling in your banana hat
not minding being simpler
lower, unimportant.

Big Snow

"Pray hard to weather, that lone surviving god,
that in some sudden wisdom we surrender."
                                                  —Richard Hugo

Driving her father's bobcat
the neighbor's daughter appears—
blonde hair, face of a goddess
dressed in Ralphie's snowsuit
from *A Christmas Story*.

A woman who retrains limbs
maps new brain paths, today
Shannon arms herself
with our red shovel, bends
down to icy drifts entombing
nine steps to our front door.

She sees snow, knows this roof
leaks, our eaves ache; we're
in deep: heart stents, arthritis.

Her boyfriend snow plows,
sends white stuff flying
big powdery piles. Through
the blizzard's fierce wind
their eyes hold a fire; lovers,
their lips do nothing but beam.

We stand in our kitchen
a team not fit to disc
watch how they clear and bow
to work that is not their own.
The snow frosts their brows;
their cheeks blush and weep.

How heavy fresh snow;
its weight bends my spine.
My husband's navy robe
predicts an early darkness.

I want to be buried on a day
when it snows and snows and snows.
From the backyard, may our dogs rise
and run. Someone, born again
into the world of stars, sleeps
waiting for me, bye and bye and bye.

AT SEVENTY

As my hair grays, I think of Mother—manic
pacing, a mare tied, bred in her stall, wild
eyed, her mind thrashing. At seventy, I've
out run her by two decades. Flashing blue

light of time hounds me and my spine's jockey
is loss. Grace Kelly, Diana, even
blonde wives of kings prick fingers, fall asleep.
Orphans become barn girls, walking, watering

brushing and braiding the mane of grief. Bare
hands break any fence to fix a splintered hub.
Skip the frame where coffin notes get pinned. Stiff
lipped, we followed the hearse, beauty's iron bed.

Think of the rag-dressed princess, her sorrel horse
who spoke the truth. Men's swords cut off his head
nailed it to a wall. Possessed, he continued to speak.
He whispered to the girl whenever she passed
and on words alone, the princess survived.

WASHING MY SISTER'S BACK

I had hardly begun when she moaned,
told me the hot water and soapy cloth
feels so good. Dank smell of sickness
lingers. Her back is thin, freckled, spent.

I can feel the weight of every pound—
her babies, toxic men, hospital work.
Beaches, NYC, where she's never been
what she's missed and carried, her spine's

crevasse ripening, wide enough to let
Covid in. There are six of us, no matter
who fills the litter, fingertips to ledge
we climb together, no safety ropes. I

don't remember a day without dread
an hour when my back pack wasn't
ready to go, boots near the bed, fear
the only fairytale we were ever read.

*In the ambulance, then the hospital
I thought I might die,* she says. Hands
stop washing for a spell and I nearly
cry when she tells me *the yellow lotion,*

all my fingers, palms tracing her ribs
reminds her of church,
our last Easter dresses, Mom's red
lipstick—how pretty she was.

What I want to say
is something about rocking
taking her into my lap and how I will
never, ever let her die.

Notes

"Call From West Virginia to Ohio, 1956" is a "Golden Shovel," a form Terrance Hayes invented in which one takes a line from a poem and uses each word in the line, in order, as the new poem's end words. The line for this poem was from Richard Hugo's "Letter to Matthews from Barton Street Flats."

The poem "Strawberries" is after Mary Oliver's poem "1945-1985: Poem for the Anniversary." The poem "Coal Miner, Caples, West Virginia, 1938" is based on the photo with the same title by Marion Post Wolcott. The poem "A Hind's Daughter" is based on the 1883 painting with the same title by the Scottish artist, Sir James Guthrie.

The poems in *No Matter How Many Windows* are based on research and stories about my great grandmother, Bertha White Stiles, whose husband deserted her and their thirteen children, my grandmother, Mary Alice Stiles, my mother, Wilma Stiles Henderson and myself.

Many of the poems in *Tenderly Lift Me: Nurses Honored, Celebrated and Remembered*, are from my creative writing thesis directed by Maggie Anderson.

The poems from *Blind Horse: Poems* tell Appalachia's outmigration story as it relates to my family and the deindustrialization saga of our town after the mill closed.

The poem "Day the Ladle's Handle Broke" is a true story, shared with me by Dr. Louis Loria years ago. A few days after I wrote this new poem, a similar accident occurred in our county.

The following poems have dedications: "Blue Lace Socks" is dedicated to Kevin Wise (1959-2020); "In Velvet" is dedicated to my sister, Sara Yost and her daughter, Florence Yvonne Michael (1966-1999); "Above All" is dedicated to Ryan Strange; "Begin in Love" is dedicated to Karen and Pat Breshnahan; "Day the Ladle's Handle Broke" is dedicated to Jawaylyn
Patterson (1994-2024); "Washing My Sister's Back" is dedicated to my sister, Nancy Henderson.

ACKNOWLEDGMENTS

I would like to thank the following publishers for originally publishing these books: *Early Farming Woman* (Finishing Line Press, 2014); *No Matter How Many Windows* (Wind Publications, 2010); *Blind Horse: Poems* (Bottom Dog Press, 1999); *Breathless* (Kent State University Press, 1995); *Tenderly Lift Me: Nurses Honored, Celebrated and Remembered* (Kent State University Press, 2004); *Smoke: Poems* (Bottom Dog Press, 2012); *Both Shoes Off* (Bottom Dog Press, 2016).

I would like to thank the following magazines/spaces where the work in *New Poems* appeared, some times in a different form or is forthcoming *Appalachian Journal*, "Call from West Virginia to Ohio, 1956," "Above All," May, 2024; *Hektoen International Journal*, "Blessed is the Heart," 2020; *Hiram Poetry Review*, "Honey," Spring, 2023; *New Limestone Review*, "Assisted Living" and "Bargaining at My Husband's Bedside, Coronary Step Down Unit, 2002," 2024; *Still: The Journal*, "Letter from the Trenches," 2019, "Washing My Sister's Back," 2024; "Frost's Farm, 1994" forthcoming in *Pine Mountain Sand & Gravel, 2024*; *Thimble Lit*, "Driving Through Amish Country, First Sunday, Family Day at the Drug Rehab," 2022; *Wild Crone Wisdom, eds. Stacy Russo, Julie Artman*, (Wild Librarian Press, 2023), "Tree" and "Midden," *Women Artists: A Celebration!: YWCA's 42nd Annual Women Artists: A Celebration*, "Blue Shirt," July, 2024.

Thanks to my husband, David, for his faith these many years and my sister, Nancy. Thanks to my parents who waved goodbye to family and the landscape they loved to row a little boat named *Hope* across Ohio's deep river. In memory of my teachers, Gloria Young, Collette Inez, Zee Edgell and Karl Patten. Deep gratitude to Vivian Pemberton and Elizabeth Hoobler who first called me a writer and poet. Maggie Anderson's guidance has been invaluable on my journey to become a better writer. For their years of attention, I thank my writing sisters, Diane Gilliam, Katherine Orr, and Alice Cone.

Before they found a publisher, the voices/stories from *Tenderly Lift Me: Nurses Honored, Celebrated and Remembered* were on stage locally and nationally as performance art thanks to Zen Campbell, Emmy Krielkamp and Nicole Pearce. I am indebted to them and Dr. Carol Donley for choosing the manuscript for the Literature and Medicine series at Hiram College. Eventually, the poems went to Edinburgh, Scotland for the 2004 Fringe Festival, Nicole Pearce, director. Later, they were performed as a ballet, thanks to Dr. Margaret Carlson, director and Dr. Martin Kohn ever a friend and mentor to my words. Gratitude for their vision and the absolute magic created with words, lighting, actors, music and dancers.

Blind Horse: Poems was submitted twenty-seven times in nine years, and a finalist four times in national contests before Larry Smith, Bottom Dog Press published it. Later, it was mounted as a staged performance art piece thanks to Russell Zampino and the Back Door Theater. It was performed for the international Working Class Studies Conference, Youngstown, OH 1997 thanks to Dr. John Russo and Dr. Sherry Linkon. Thanks to all for their friendship, encouragement and faith in my work.

Eternal gratitude to Robert Wick and Walter Wick for generously supporting poetry through their Wick Poetry Foundation at Kent State University and to Jack Stadler's support for poetry fellowships at Bucknell University. Working with Collette Inez and Karl Patten was unforgettable. The first Ohio Arts Council fellowship gave me a chance to have sabbatical, continue with research for *Tenderly Lift Me* and complete it. The second OAC grant provided me with time to finish a short story collection. I am thankful for both awards and leaves granted to me by nursing supervisors, Helen Banks and Lois McClain. Much gratitude to Vermont Studio Center for the fellowship and residency which provided space to write many of the poems for *No Matter How Many Windows* and fellow artist, Mary Connelly, for her beautiful painting, "Blue Plate", and to Susan Jacobs for her lovely painting, "Homage to a Shirt" used on the cover of this book.

ABOUT THE AUTHOR

Jeanne Bryner's family was part of Appalachia's outmigration from Wetzel County, West Virginia and Greene County, Pennsylvania. Following work, her parents moved to Ohio where her father was hired in a mill. Migration and the fracture of family is never easy. "Home is the landscape familiar to one's heart and speech patterns gathering on evening's porch."

Due to family illness, she has been a caregiver her entire life. Another layer of migration is the absence of extended family. "The bodies around you are the ones you lean against; they are your life vest, even if they are babies."

She grew up in Newton Falls, Ohio. A retired board certified emergency room nurse, she's a graduate of Trumbull Memorial Hospital's School of Nursing and Kent State University's Honors College. She has several books in print and her work has been adapted for the stage nationally and also the 2005 Fringe Festival in Edinburgh, Scotland. She has received awards for community service, nursing, and writing fellowships from Bucknell University, the Ohio Arts Council (1997, 2007) and Vermont Studio Center.

With Cortney Davis, she co-edited *Learning to Heal: Reflections on Nursing School in Poetry and Prose*, Kent State University Press, 2018 which received the Tillie Olsen Award for creative writing from the Working Class Studies Association and 2019 American Journal of Nursing Book of the Year Award for creative writing. In 2012 her book, *Smoke: Poems*, Bottom Dog Press, received an AJN Book of the Year award for creative writing. Her book, *No Matter How Many Windows,* Wind Publications, received the 2011 WCSA Tillie Olsen Award for creative writing. In 2022 with the support of Sigma's International Nurse Honor Society chapter, Delta Xi, she established a Nurse Honor Guard unit in her community.

Jeanne lives near a dairy farm with her husband David, a veteran and retired die setter. Her son works in a machine shop and her daughter is a nurse.

BOOKS BY BOTTOM DOG
WORKING LIVES SERIES

In Velevet: New & Selected Poems 1995-2024, Jeanne Bryner, 202 pgs, $18
Wanted: Good Family: A Novel, Joseph G. Anthony, 212 pgs, $17
A Wounded Snake: A Novel, Joseph G. Anthony, 264 pgs, $18
Lake Effect: Poems, Laura Treacy Bentley, 108 pgs, $14
Smoke: Poems, Jeanne Bryner, 96 pgs, $16
Eclipse: Stories, Jeanne Bryner, 150 pgs, $16
Blind Horse: Poems, Jeanne Bryner, 100 pgs, $16
Cycling Through Columbine, J.R.W. Case, 264 pgs, $18
Brown Bottle: A Novel, Sheldon Lee Compton, 160 pgs, $17
No Pets: Stories, Jim Ray Daniels, 134 pgs, $16
Story Hour & Other Stories, Robert Flanagan, 104 pgs, $15
Salvatore & Maria, Finding Paradise, Paul L. Gentile, 247 pgs, $18
Earnest Occupations, Richard Hague, 200 pgs, $18
Learning How: Stories, Tales & Yarns, Richard Hague, 206 pgs, $16
A Small Room With Trouble on My Mind and Other Stories,
Michael Henson, 160 pgs, $17
Pottery Town, Karen Kotrba, 130 pgs, $16
Beautiful Rust: Poems, Ken Meisel, 96 pgs
In Plena Vita- The Full Life: The Collected Poems of Timothy Russell, 280 pgs, $20
Waiting at the Dead End Diner: Poems, Rebecca Schumejda, 204 pgs, $17
The Free Farm: A Novel, Larry Smith, 306 pgs, $17
The Long River Home: A Novel, by Larry Smith,
230 pgs, cloth $22; paper $16
Mingo Town & Memories, Larry Smith, 94 pgs, $15
Milldust and Roses: Memoirs, Larry Smith, 149 pgs, $12
Beyond Rust: Novella & Stories, Larry Smith, 156 pgs
A River Remains: Poems, Larry Smith, 236 pgs,
Yeoman's Work: Poems, Garrett Stack, 92 pgs, $16
Drone String: Poems, Sherry Cook Stanforth, 92 pgs, $16
Choices: Three Novellas, Annabel Thomas, 180 pgs, $18
The Country Doctor's Wife: Memoirs, Cornelia Cattell Thompson,
166 pgs, $18
Voices From the Appalachian Coalfields, Mike Yarrow & Ruth Yarrow,
Photos by Douglas Yarrow, 152 pgs, $17

Bottom Dog Press, Inc.
P.O. Box 425 /Huron, Ohio 44839
http://smithdocs.net

Books by Bottom Dog Press
Appalachian Writing Series

Labor Days, Labor Nights: More Stories, Larry D. Thacker, 208 pgs, $18

The Long Way Home, Ron Lands, 170 pgs, $18

40 Patchtown: A Novel, Damian Dressick, 184 pgs, $18

Mama's Song, P. Shaun Neal, 238 pgs, $18

Fissures and Other Stories, by Timothy Dodd, 152 pgs, $18

Old Brown, by Craig Paulenich, 92 pgs, $16

Sky Under the Roof: Poems, by Hilda Downer, 126 pgs, $16

Green-Silver and Silent: Poems, by Marc Harshman, 90 pgs, $16

The Homegoing: A Novel, by Michael Olin-Hitt, 180 pgs, $18

She Who Is Like a Mare: Poems of Mary Breckinridge and the Frontier Nursing Service, by Karen Kotrba, 96 pgs, $16

Broken Collar: A Novel, by Ron Mitchell, 234 pgs, $18

The Pattern Maker's Daughter: Poems, by Sandee Gertz Umbach, 90 pgs, $16

Sinners of Sanction County: Stories, by Charles Dodd White, 160 pgs, $17

Working Lives & Appalachian Writing Series Anthologies

Unbroken Circle: Stories of Cultural Diversity in the South, Eds. Julia Watts and Larry Smith, 194 pgs, $18

Appalachia Now: Short Stories of Contemporary Appalachia, Eds. Charles Dodd White and Larry Smith, 178 pgs, $18

Degrees of Elevation: Short Stories of Contemporary Appalachia, Eds. Charles Dodd White and Page Seay, 186 pgs, $18

Appalachia Now: Short Stories of Contemporary Appalachia, Eds. Charles Dodd White and Larry Smith, 178 pgs, $17

Working Hard for the Money: America's Working Poor in Stories, Poems and Photos, Eds. Mary E. Weems & Larry Smith, 204 pgs, $12

On the Clock: Contemporary Short Stories of Work, Eds, Jeff Vande Zande & John Maday, 188 pgs, $15

Writing Work: Writers on Working-Class Writing, Eds. David Shevin, Larry Smith, Janet Zandy, 220 pgs, $15

Free Shipping.
http://smithdocs.net